LI

IN

LONDON

A Practical Guide

THE JUNIOR LEAGUE OF LONDON

JUNIOR LEAGUE OF
LONDON

ISBN-13: 9781677683215

CONTENTS

JUNIOR LEAGUE OF LONDON

ABOUT US

The Junior League of London (JLL) has served the London community since 1978. **Our mission is simple: to promote voluntary service, develop the potential of women and improve our community through the effective action and leadership of trained volunteers.** We partner with charities, schools and community centres who share the vision of combating poverty in London.

In 1981, the first edition of Living in London was published. Now in its twelfth edition, the information has changed, but our purpose has not. This publication is created by our members to share valuable information about moving, transitioning and thriving in the UK.

JLL is a non-profit organisation and proceeds of

this book fund our volunteers in leadership training, support service programs for our action areas and promote our mission. We appreciate your purchase and hope this makes your Living in London experience brilliant!

To learn more about the JLL and how you can get involved in our mission, visit our website: jll.org.uk.

Cheers,

Members of The Junior League of London

Chapter 1:

Moving

Moving to London from abroad can be a daunting and often confusing experience. Though the language might be familiar, the culture can seem quite foreign. For many, navigating the move can easily prove overwhelming. Many of the systems and processes you may be accustomed to at home are different in the UK. Therefore, it is important to do your homework and begin planning well in advance. In particular, it is essential that you and your family have the appropriate visas, work permits and/or other documentation needed for entry into the country. The following pages highlight some points to consider prior to relocating to the UK, as well as providing helpful tips for preparing and making the move much easier.

CLIMATE AND WEATHER

Weather in London is unpredictable, but extreme conditions are rare. The average temperature varies from a low of 0°C (32°F) to a high of 24°C (about 75°F). July is the warmest month, while January is the coldest. One common climate condition is a very light drizzle, so carrying a brolly (umbrella) and wearing water-resistant outerwear is almost always a good idea. And don't forget to pack your wellies (Wellington boots/rain boots)! You will find that it can get quite cool at night, even in summer, and carrying a sweater or light jacket is advisable.

Temperatures are usually reported in Celsius. For an approximate conversion from Celsius to Fahrenheit, double the Celsius temperature and add 30. Or use this easy reference!

CELSIUS (CENTIGRADE) TO FAHRENHEIT

°C	°F
-5	23.0
-1	30.2
0	32.0 (freezing point)
1	33.8

5	41.0
10	50.0
15	59.0
20	68.0
25	77.0
30	86.0
37	98.6 (average human body temperature)
100	212.0 (boiling point)

IMMIGRATION

Before moving to the UK, you must ensure that you have been granted permission from the British government. Depending on your nationality and the purpose and length of your stay, you may need to obtain a visa before entering the country. Please note that most people travelling to the UK for more than six months must obtain entry clearance before arriving.

Information regarding immigration law is often the subject of rumours so be certain that the advice you receive is from a reliable source. If you are moving due to your job, your company's Human Resources department often organises the process for you. Be wary if you are asked to seek independent advice. If your adviser is not a lawyer, solicitor, barrister or legal executive, you should ensure he or she is authorised by the Office of the Immigration Services Commissioner (OISC). A list of OISC-authorised advisers is available from the OISC. The office can be reached through oisc.gov.uk.

You may also wish to seek advice from the British consulate or diplomatic post nearest to you. The Foreign and Commonwealth Office (fco.gov.uk) lists all UK diplomatic missions around the world. In addition, embassies often have a list of attorneys practising in the UK who can assist with immigration matters.

ENTRY CLEARANCE (VISAS AND WORK PERMITS)

Entry clearance in the form of visas and work permits is constantly evolving and it is recommended that you seek advice for your specific situation. The Home Office is the first place to begin your enquiries: gov.uk (search *Immigration*).

MOVING YOUR BELONGINGS

When selecting an overseas moving company, choose a reputable one. Investigate the company's performance record and check references. Go over all items in detail with the moving company's representative and ensure you have everything in writing. Get more than one estimate. Do not choose a firm simply because it is the cheapest; it may turn out to be a 'penny wise, pound foolish' decision. If you are moving abroad for work, your employer may have a list of preferred carriers. Do not be afraid to ask questions about the process and make sure that you receive copies of all important documents.

Air versus sea

You may have the option of shipping your goods via air and/or sea. Air shipments usually take one to two weeks and are typically the most expensive method. Sea shipments will likely be in a container and normally arrive within four to six weeks. If you are moving abroad for work, your employer may specify a certain-sized container. Make sure you ask about the specifics before scheduling any estimates.

If you are shipping via sea, you should know which ship is going to carry your container and when it is scheduled to depart for and arrive in the UK. Upon arrival, your moving company should make arrangements with HM Revenue & Customs and the UK removal company that will transfer your shipment from the port to your home. Goods can take anywhere between a few days to a couple of weeks to clear customs. Ensure that you have the appropriate contact information for each step of the journey.

Insurance and inventory

You should be familiar with moving and removal companies' loss and damage protection policies – read all the small print before signing any contract. It is essential to have insurance. Your local homeowner's policy will not cover your belongings once they leave port so be sure to know the scope and coverage of the insurance for the shipment. It might be wise to check with one or more private insurance companies instead of relying on the moving company's insurance programme.

For insurance purposes, it is necessary to have an itemised inventory. This list might be done by categories (e.g. furniture, silver, paintings, and accessories) or by each room in your home. Pick the system that best suits your needs and remember to value all items at replacement value. It is a good idea to have everything appraised and to record everything with photographs.

Make several copies of your inventory. One copy must go to the insuring company, which may be the moving company or a separate insurance agent.

Take more than one copy with you when the shipment arrives in the UK. This inventory list makes it easy to record any possible damage which might require repair and an insurance claim. If possible, be present when your goods are unpacked at your home. Raise any insurance claims quickly as most policies do not permit claims once a certain amount of time has passed.

Shipping household items

Deciding which household items to bring with you depends on many factors, including the anticipated length of your stay and your accommodation. A complete move can take several months to arrange while a temporary or short-term move can happen almost immediately. If possible, try to schedule a house-hunting trip to view different types of properties before you move (see *Chapter 2: Housing* for information about London neighbourhoods and searching for properties).

UK houses and flats typically have little storage space both inside and outside. If you are planning on renting accommodation in London, keep in mind that many rental flats and houses are fully furnished (this may include dishes, sheets, towels, etc.). Storage units are often expensive so you should consider beforehand how your household items will fit into your new home.

Start by making lists:

- What is going with you on the airplane?

- What is needed soon after you arrive? If you are moving into temporary housing, it may be necessary to bring these items with you as excess baggage or via an air shipment.

- What is being shipped in a container via sea/air?

- What is going into storage?

- Do you have any items to give away, sell or discard?

Once you have made all of these decisions, it is a good idea to have the lists duplicated so that you are protected in case you lose a copy.

DID YOU KNOW?

When choosing items to bring, it is important to remember that many flats are converted 19th-century homes. While they are certainly beautiful, their narrow hallways, doors and staircases may not accommodate large pieces of furniture. Make sure your removal company is aware of any large items – it may need to hire a crane to lift furniture through windows or rooftop patio doors.

Packing your household

Make sure your specifications and instructions are carried out to your satisfaction. Ensure that each and every box is labelled with its contents and destination. If you are doing any of the packing or unpacking, check for insurance coverage. Generally, breakable items are only covered when packed and unpacked by the moving company. Shipping charges normally include all packing and unpacking.

What to bring

Deciding what to bring when you move to London is an individual decision. Obviously, your decisions will be based on the anticipated length of time you will reside in the UK. It will also depend upon your housing – whether furnished or unfurnished, house or flat.

The following items may not be readily available or easily replaced in the UK. If they are available in the UK, they may be considerably more expensive than they are abroad.

Personal items

- Medical prescriptions may be branded differently. Ask your doctor or pharmacist for the name of the underlying compound to ensure that you receive the same medicine when you fill your prescriptions in the UK.

- Any over-the-counter medicine that you particularly like. There are many brands that are unavailable in the UK, including many from the United States.

- Eyeglasses, contact lenses, and related products.

- Special cosmetics and beauty products, particularly dermatologist-recommended ones.

For the home

- European and UK beds and bedding vary greatly in size from those sold elsewhere, particularly in the United States, and are relatively expensive. If you bring your own beds, you should also bring appropriate bedding.

- British recipes use imperial and metric measurements and some UK measuring utensils differ in size from those sold elsewhere. To ensure that you can make your recipes in the UK, you may wish to bring a set of measuring cups and spoons along with your favourite cookbooks. For cooking tips and measurement conversion tables, see *Chapter 10: Cooking, food and drink*.

Miscellaneous

- Children's games, sports equipment (baseballs, softballs, bats, footballs, basketballs and bicycles).

- Special decorations for various holidays that you celebrate throughout the year.

On the plane

- Bring copies of any important legal documents with you. Make a full copy of your passport and any visa or work permit information.

- Copies of any wills, insurance policies, rental contracts on properties and investments and a list of current charge accounts with their account numbers. Make sure a trusted friend or attorney knows the whereabouts of the originals.

- Copies of family medical records.

- Sewing kit, small first-aid kit, extra pair of glasses, extra prescriptions, small toolkit, some old clothes for cleaning or painting, and a set of linens.

- Jewellery.

What not to bring

- Cordless telephones.

- Light bulbs (except appliance bulbs – see *Electrical appliances* in this chapter for an explanation of electrical differences).

- Christmas tree lights.

- Electric clocks (if moving from the Americas or Japan).

- Liquor/spirits (excluding wine), except duty-free allowances.

- Cigarettes, except duty-free allowances.

- Perfumes, except duty-free allowances.

- Paints, cleaning agents, or other combustible or flammable items.

- Plants and bulbs.

- Meat, fruit, and vegetables.

- Certain fish and eggs.

- Most animals and all birds (except pets – see *Bringing your pet to the UK* in this chapter).

- Items made from protected species, including reptile leather, ivory, and fur skins.

HM Revenue & Customs has a set of frequently asked questions and information on what not to bring on their website: hmrc.gov.uk.

DID YOU KNOW?

Laws on bringing decorative sports equipment and firearms for sports purposes into the UK are extremely restrictive. You are advised to check the current law when you move.

Customs and VAT

The British government allows the import of all household or personal items duty-free if they have been owned for at least six months prior to the date of entry into the UK. Proof of purchase must be available on items less than six months old. Certain other household items may be subject to duty charges. There are also special regulations regarding the import of inherited goods and antiques. Excise taxes are payable on certain items such as liquor and cigarettes.

If possible, maintain a file with a copy of the bills of sale for every valuable item owned including cameras, watches, jewellery, silver, major appliances, etc. If you do not have the bill of sale, a copy of an insurance policy that itemises the articles can be used. Carry these documents with you. Do not ship them.

All items that are not at least six months old are subject to duty charges and VAT (value added tax, which is currently 20 per cent on most goods). Check with your moving company regarding which items may be subject to duty and excise tax plus VAT as these can vary depending on the item in question. For additional information, visit the HM Revenue & Customs website: hmrc.gov.uk.

Electrical appliances

Deciding which electrical appliances and equipment to bring to the UK or leave at home can be confusing, especially if you are relocating from North America. The UK (and most of Europe) has an electrical supply of 220/240 volts and 50 Hz (frequency or cycles per second) while the North American supply is 110 volts and 60 Hz.

Understanding which voltage and frequency is compatible with your electrical devices will facilitate your decision-making. Some devices, if designed for several voltages, can be used directly in the UK with a plug adaptor. Others can be used with a voltage transformer and some cannot be used at all. Given the expense of adaptors and transformers (and the shortage of space in most London flats) you may find it easier to purchase smaller appliances after settling into your new home.

Adaptors

Most UK plugs have three rectangular prongs. Electrical devices that do not need voltage transformers can be used with a plug adaptor. Alternatively, a non-UK plug can be replaced with a UK plug. While the latter option is cheaper, be sure to ask an electrician or local hardware store (e.g. B&Q, diy.com) if you are unsure of how to replace the plugs.

Transformers

In general, most non-European electrical goods are incompatible with UK electrical supply because of the voltage difference (220/240V for UK versus 110V for North America, for example). This means they will burn out if you try to use them in the UK. They may work if you use a transformer, which is a plug-in device that will convert 220/240V to 110V. Transformers are available in hardware and electrical shops in most major UK towns or online.

They are sized between 30 watts and 1,500 watts with prices ranging accordingly. A hair dryer or electric curler will require up to a 250-watt transformer. A blender or food processor will require up to a 500-watt transformer, while a refrigerator will require up to a 1,500-watt transformer.

Depending on their size, transformers can be used to power several appliances – meaning you do not necessarily need a transformer for each device. It is worth noting that transformers are bulky and heavy so are not very portable.

Dual voltage appliances

Some appliances – such as cameras, home computers, printers, video recorders, televisions and stereos – are dual voltage and can function on 120V/60Hz or 240V/50Hz. The appliance may automatically adjust to the correct voltage. Otherwise, a switch on the appliance may need to be adjusted. Check the label on your appliance or the owner's manual for this feature. If it is dual voltage, you are able to use it in the UK without a transformer.

DID YOU KNOW?

Most laptops and mobile device chargers can be used in the UK with an adaptor. However, it is always wise to check the label to verify that the device is rated for 240V & 50Hz.

Incompatible appliances

The electrical supply in most of the world, including the UK, is 50Hz. However, the supply is 60Hz in North America and parts of South America and Japan. This frequency difference is significant in motorised appliances where the speed of the motor is important. There is no simple device that will convert 60Hz to 50Hz so any device with a motor will run at just over 80 per cent of its normal speed when using a transformer. For hair dryers and fans, that will probably be OK. For larger, more powerful items such as washers, blenders, refrigerators and dryers, it could prove to be a problem. It will be an issue for analogue clocks.

The frequency difference is not an issue when using certain devices with motors, such as video recorders, personal computers and audio equipment. This is because the electrical current is automatically converted to Direct Current in the machine, so the device will run at the right speed – independent of frequency.

Specific appliances

Refrigerator

A refrigerator can be run on an appropriately-sized transformer. North American-sized refrigerators may be purchased in the UK. If you are renting and wish to have a large refrigerator, make sure there is space in the kitchen to accommodate one since British refrigerators are often small.

Washing machines and electric dryers

A washer can be run on an appropriately-sized transformer. The dryer will likely be 240V and may work without a transformer. We recommend consulting with a qualified electrician prior to installation. North American washers and dryers are larger than UK appliances and may not fit in your particular house or flat. If you wish to have larger appliances, ensure that you have adequate space for them. Gas dryers can be used in the UK if your flat or house has a gas supply. However, they will need a transformer for the motor and may need a different pressure regulator for the gas.

Televisions, DVD/Blu-Ray, home entertainment

If you want to bring your television, DVD/Blu-Ray player, gaming system and other home entertainment devices, first check the label and user's manual. If it is dual voltage, then it should work with a plug adaptor.

If you have a newer digital television (less than 3-5 years old), you should not have a problem receiving local television programming. If you have an older, non-digital television, it may not be able to display local UK programming without a switch and specialised set-up. Similarly, an American DVD/Blu-Ray player will not play UK videos unless it is a region free or multi-region machine.

It may be wise to sell these appliances before moving to the UK and buy new or used ones once you arrive.

DID YOU KNOW?

DVDs are coded differently for different regions of the world. For example, North America is coded as Zone 1. Europe and Japan are coded as Zone 2 and South America is coded as Zone 4. If you are bringing your DVDs, make sure the DVD player you purchase in the UK is multi-regional and can play DVDs from the appropriate zone. Likewise, do not buy DVDs in the UK and expect to be able to play them when you return home. Blu-Rays can also have coding, but do not follow the same zones as DVDs.

If you happen to be addicted to television programming in your home country, consider getting a streaming device, service or try Slingbox (slingbox.com). Slingbox is connected to your cable/satellite box in your home country and streams the television programming to your computer. It is easy to buy cables in the UK to connect your computer to your television. However, most North American television programmes are shown on British television within months of appearing in the United States.

Telephones

North American landline telephones are not compatible with the UK system, although some telephones may be used in the UK after purchasing an adaptor. However, the price of an adaptor may be more expensive than the price of a new phone. Therefore, it is not advisable to bring landline telephones to the UK.

Computers

Most computers are dual voltage and can function as either 120V or 240V. However, your computer accessories (e.g. speakers and printers) may not be. Check the label on the unit and power cord or review your user manual. If they are not dual voltage, your computer, monitor and printer will run on a transformer in the UK. You can purchase a surge protector when you arrive in the UK.

Lamps

All lamps (except those using halogen or fluorescent bulbs) can be used in the UK if they are used with an adaptor or are fitted with UK plugs. 110V light bulbs will explode if used in the UK because of the voltage difference, so you may leave your light bulbs at home or plug the lamp into a transformer. The ballast in halogen lamps must be changed and may be difficult to find.

Miscellaneous electrical information

If you have electrical appliances that require appliance bulbs such as sewing machines, refrigerators and freezers, bring the bulbs with you. For your electrical questions and needs, contact Ryness Lighting & Electrical (ryness.co.uk) or your local electrical/hardware shop.

DID YOU KNOW?

If you plan to rent accommodation, keep in mind that most flats and houses come furnished with basic appliances.

Bringing your pet to the UK

To guard against the importation of rabies and other animal diseases, the Department of Environment, Food & Rural Affairs (DEFRA) requires a four-to-six-month quarantine for cats, dogs, and other rabies-susceptible animals coming into the UK. It may be possible to bring your pet into the country without quarantine under the Pet Travel Scheme (PETS). PETS only applies to certain types of domestic animals (dogs, cats, and ferrets) arriving from certain countries and only if they meet certain requirements. If you are planning to take your pets to the UK through the scheme, begin the process approximately eight months before you expect to move to ensure that your pet will not have to spend any time in quarantine. The scheme requires a substantial amount of paperwork and co-ordination with both your local veterinarian and the local agricultural authority in your home country. It is extremely important that all procedures are explicitly adhered to in the precise order instructed. Failure to do so may result in your pet not being admitted to the UK and a requirement to restart the process. DEFRA has extensive information about the PETS programme and the pet passport, including forms and checklists. Visit the DEFRA website for the most up-to-date forms and requirements: defra.gov.uk.

A brief outline of the necessary steps:

• You must microchip your pet and verify that the microchip can be read by standard scanners.

• A 21-day waiting period is required after a rabies booster and a health certificate must be issued within 10 days of travel. Please see this website for specific requirements by country of origin:

gov.uk/take-pet-abroad/rabies-vaccination-boosters-and- blood-tests.

• Immediately before entering the UK, your pet must receive tick and tapeworm treatment and all paperwork must be correctly completed.

• As well as complying with the PETS programme, you must arrange for your pet's transportation. The scheme requires that your pet enter the country using an approved transport company and route (a list of which can be found on DEFRA's website). You must purchase a carrier for your pet that meets the airline's kennel guidelines and labelling requirements (this information is usually available on each airline's website. Kennels can be purchased from the airline or a pet supply store). Note that the guidelines are strictly enforced and the airline can and will refuse to ship your pet if the guidelines are not adhered to.

• Most airlines also require a certificate of acclimation from your veterinarian and a statement regarding food and water from the pet owner. The certificate of acclimation states that your pet can fly at certain temperatures. It can only be obtained 24 to 48 hours before departure. This certificate can be problematic if you are travelling during very high or very low temperatures. Check with your airline for any additional documentation they may require from the veterinarian as some require the veterinarian to declare within 48 hours of the flight that the pet is in good health to fly. These forms can be completed by the veterinarian at the same time as the tapeworm process.

• You must complete a customs form for your pet to ensure that it will clear customs upon arrival in the UK. Most airlines require a broker to clear pets through customs and can often provide these services if asked. If they cannot, call customs or DEFRA for more information. Note that it is essential to clarify your point of entry (e.g. Heathrow, Gatwick or another UK airport) to ensure the broker is at the airport where you will arrive. You must have all the original documentation as copies are not accepted.

• If your pet is arriving in the UK by one of the approved airlines, the airline will transfer your pet to the Animal Reception Centre at the airport. It is there that your pet's paperwork will be examined. You will need to collect your pet from the Centre. Note that it is often located far from the terminals with little or no public transportation available. Having or renting a car is recommended.

For a more complete listing of the current quarantine requirements and travel procedures, including approved quarantine premises and carrying agents, visit DEFRA's website.

DID YOU KNOW?

Several breeds of dogs are not permitted in the UK including pit bulls. It is important to check the list of dog breeds permitted by DEFRA. If there is any question as to the dog's breed or it is unknown, a behaviour test will be performed or you can have a relatively inexpensive DNA test completed by mail order.

Flying with your pet

Travelling with a pet can be very expensive. The price of your pet's ticket varies by airline but may be determined by the size of the carrier or the combined weight of the carrier and the pet. Your approved carrier may require you to travel on the same flight as your pet. If this is the case, check with the airline to understand when a reservation can be made for your pet as your pet's flight usually needs to be booked by the airline's cargo division. It is recommended that you do not book your flight until you have confirmed with the cargo division that there is space available for the pet. Most airlines' cargo space has a special environmentally-controlled segment for pets. You may want to book space in this area well in advance.

Resources

If your employer is handling your moving arrangements, enquire about their resources and make sure that the costs of your pet's move will also be covered. In the event that your pet must be quarantined in the UK, arrangements for boarding kennels must be made and confirmed by letter before you leave your home. Allow at least four to six weeks to complete all associated paperwork and keep in mind that the most accessible kennels may have waiting lists.

While it is possible for you to navigate the Pet Travel Scheme on your own, companies offer services that make it easier for you. These include:

- Passport for Pets: passportforpets.co.uk
- Pet Relocation: petrelocation.com (For animals moving from the United States)

DID YOU KNOW?

Penalties for smuggling animals are severe. Such an offence will result in a heavy fine, a prison sentence for yourself or the destruction of the animal.

Arriving at the airport

There are five airports in London but you will most likely arrive at Heathrow Airport or Gatwick Airport. Depending on the terminal, it is often a long walk from the gates to passport control. Therefore, if you require a wheelchair, are travelling with a young child or have medical problems, you should pre-arrange special assistance with your airline or plan accordingly.

Once at passport control, join the correct queue (line) as per your current citizenship. You will be asked to submit a completed landing card given to you on the flight (or at passport control) and you'll need to list the address you'll be staying at. The immigration officer may ask to see your travel documents or work permit so that he or she can stamp your passport accordingly. He or she may also ask you a few questions regarding the reasons for your entrance into the country. If you are moving for the purpose of work or study, be sure to have all relevant documents with you including offer letters, contracts, certificates of study completion and details of your contacts in the UK.

Once you are through passport control, check the electronic board for your flight's baggage claim area. In the UK and in many other European international airports, luggage trolleys are usually offered free of charge. If some or all of your luggage does not arrive, contact a representative of your airline before leaving the airport.

Customs

Once you have collected your luggage, proceed through customs. The belongings you are allowed to bring into the UK, both taxable and duty-free, depend on where you've come from, your immigration status and how long you've owned them. For additional information, visit HM Revenue & Customs' website: hmrc.gov.uk.

If you have items to declare, you must go to the area marked with the red sign. The customs inspector will likely ask you a few questions and may ask to see these items. You are required to pay any duty or tax at the time the belongings are brought into the country so be sure to travel with UK currency.

Foreign currency

Foreign currency or travellers' cheques can be exchanged for cash at airport banks. There are also cash machines (ATMs) available in most airports, which will automatically dispense UK currency. These can often be found in the baggage claim or arrivals area. It is often cheaper and easier to use cash machines. Check with your bank beforehand regarding your PIN number and whether you will incur any fees for using foreign cash machines.

Moving within London

Moving within London can sometimes be just as much of a hassle as moving to the UK. Some things to remember are:

- If you need to secure parking for unloading or loading a lorry or van, contact your local council at least two weeks ahead of time. Your local council will block parking spaces for you for free or for a small fee. For more information regarding your local council, please refer to *Chapter 5: Utilities – Local Councils*.

- You will need to transfer your TV licence to your new home (tvlicensing.co.uk) and cancel all direct debits for services to your former home.

- Try to set up services (e.g. cable and telephone) before moving into your new home.

- Royal Mail offers a redirection service (royalmail.com). For a fee, they will forward all your mail – including magazines and parcels – to your new address in the UK or abroad for up to two years. Any local post office will have the request forms.

When hiring a removals company, be sure to check references and enquire about insurance limits. Many removals companies will move boxes that you have packed yourself, which can be less expensive than purchasing a full moving service. Prices are sometimes lower if you move during the week rather than on a weekend.

Chapter 2:

Housing

What makes London such a wonderfully liveable city is that it is made up of many small villages, each with its own particular charm. Deciding on the best location for you and your family is difficult only because the choice is so vast. You must consider a number of factors: the high cost of living in certain areas, proximity to work and schools (or easy transportation to them), convenience of shopping facilities and atmosphere. If it is at all possible, any house-hunting trip should begin with a day spent travelling around the city to take in the flavour and overall feel of each area.

If you are new to the London area, find an experienced guide to take you around the city. Your relocation/estate agent as well as black cab or minicab companies are good sources. By the time your tour ends, your list of areas in which to search for housing may be considerably shorter. Once you have narrowed down your preferences, it is also wise to revisit the area after dark. Darkness falls very early in the winter and you should make sure you are comfortable in the area even after nightfall. Those few hours of touring can save you days of wasted time and energy, not to mention frayed nerves.

The first decision to make is whether you want to live in central London, in one of the suburban communities in the greater London area or further out in the countryside. London stretches across some 30 miles and is divided into 32 areas, each with its own council providing local public services such as street cleaning, social housing, libraries and parking. To pay for these services, each area sets its own level of local council tax (*see Council tax* in this chapter), which can vary significantly even between neighbouring areas. For example, the boroughs of the City of Westminster and Wandsworth have very low council tax rates while the boroughs of Islington, Camden and Kensington and Chelsea have much higher council tax rates. There are also differences in the quality of services which are mostly run by individual councils.

Parking within London can be challenging and violators will receive a fine or worse – have their vehicle clamped or towed. Certain London neighbourhoods or boroughs (notably the City of Westminster and Kensington and Chelsea) only offer metered parking to visitors. Other boroughs offer visitor passes to residents that can be used on an hourly basis or for an entire day. If you own a car, you must purchase a resident parking permit from your local council that allows you to park in designated residential areas.

LONDON NEIGHBOURHOODS

The following brief descriptions of some popular areas in London may be of assistance.

Central London (SW and W postcodes)

The communities of central London are expensive but conveniently located near shops, theatres, restaurants, clubs and public transportation. They also generally allow for a shorter commute to work in the City and other parts of central London.

These areas have a high proportion of international residents. While many have good access to tube stations, those areas with fewer tube stations often compensate by being extremely well connected by bus.

Belgravia (SW1)

Near Buckingham Palace and Hyde Park, this area consists of magnificent Regency squares, late Georgian terraces and mews houses. Some of the larger houses are now used as embassies and consulates while others have been divided into flats. Belgravia is one of the most expensive areas of London and, like Mayfair, supermarkets are limited in size and therefore provide a limited selection of goods. This area is served by Victoria and Sloane Square tube stations.

Chelsea (SW3 and SW10)

South of Knightsbridge, South Kensington and bordering the Thames, Chelsea features a range of mostly low-rise period buildings including Victorian cottages and mansion blocks. Sloane Square and King's Road are convenient for shopping, although the latter's reputation as one of London's trendiest areas is now more tradition than fact. Chelsea also boasts many cosy local pubs and restaurants as well as excellent antique shops and markets. The area is not particularly well served by public transport as there is no tube station beyond Sloane Square. There are, however, multiple bus routes that provide good access around the city.

Kensington (W8)

South and west of Kensington Gardens, Kensington features tree-lined residential streets and squares, a mixture of Georgian and Victorian terraced houses, red-brick mansion blocks and elegant villas. Kensington High Street and Notting Hill Gate stations offer convenient shopping and access to public transport. There are also numerous cinemas, restaurants and pubs in the area.

Knightsbridge (SW1, SW3 and SW7)

Bordering the south side of Hyde Park, this expensive area features Victorian terraces and squares, cobbled mews, red-brick Victorian mansion blocks and new builds. Once part of a forest on the outskirts of London, Knightsbridge today is home to Harrods, Harvey Nichols and other fine stores, making it one of the world's most famous shopping destinations. Knightsbridge tube station is on the Piccadilly line, serving the West End and Heathrow.

Marylebone (W1)

North of Oxford Street and south of Marylebone Road, this area has many 18th-century streets and squares, mews houses and Edwardian mansion blocks with a porter (doorman). It is conveniently located near the West End shops and boasts excellent public transport links to the City as well as to nearly all of London's mainline rail stations. Marylebone High Street has become a fashionable spot for shopping and has many excellent restaurants and pubs. Regent's Park is also nearby. Marylebone is served by the Baker Street, Bond Street and Regent's Park tube stations.

Mayfair (W1)

Bordered by Hyde Park, Oxford Street, Regent Street and Piccadilly, Mayfair has been a fashionable central neighbourhood since the 1700s. Many of the large Georgian houses have been divided into flats or have been converted into luxury hotels and offices. There is a good supply of flats in large, well-maintained mansion blocks. The area is limited for grocery shopping (the local custom of daily shopping still prevails). However, it is well situated near many of the finest clubs, restaurants, antique shops and designer boutiques. The area is served by the Oxford Street, Piccadilly Circus, Hyde Park Corner, Green Park and Marble Arch stations.

Pimlico (SW1)

South of Victoria Station and bordering the Thames, this area has lovely white stucco squares and terraces. Its tranquillity owes much to the complicated one-way street system. Pimlico is a more affordable alternative to the neighbouring communities of Belgravia and Chelsea and is popular with members of Parliament and other government workers based in Westminster. Pimlico is served by Pimlico and Victoria stations.

South Kensington (SW3, SW5 and SW7)

South Kensington's streets feature large terraced houses, many of which are converted into flats and often with access to private garden squares. One of the most central residential areas in London, South Kensington benefits from plentiful tube and bus services providing easy access to the West End, the City and Heathrow Airport. The area is also home to four of the capital's major museums as well as the

Lycée Français, which attracts many French families to the area. It is serviced by the South Kensington and Gloucester Road stations.

West London (W postcodes)

In addition to the west/central neighbourhoods listed below, westward from Knightsbridge are the residential areas of Brook Green, Chiswick, Hammersmith, Shepherd's Bush and West Kensington. These contain tree-lined streets with large houses, many of which have been converted into flats. The neighbourhoods are well served by public transport with the Central, Piccadilly and District lines. They are also situated on the right side of London to allow for a quick journey on the M4 motorway to Heathrow Airport. With riverside walks, pubs and excellent facilities for shopping, leisure and health, this area is ideal for families planning to settle in London for a considerable amount of time.

Bayswater and Paddington (W2)

West of Marble Arch and to the north of Hyde Park, this area possesses modern blocks of flats as well as some squares mostly rebuilt after the war. It is conveniently situated for Oxford Street shopping and Mayfair as well as being considerably cheaper than neighbouring Notting Hill. Paddington is nearby, which has benefited from the wide-scale development and urban regeneration of Paddington Basin. Paddington station hosts the Heathrow Express rail link, while the area also contains some very pretty period cottages and magnificent stucco terraces. The area is serviced by the Bayswater, Paddington and Edgware Road Stations.

Holland Park (W11 and W14)

Surrounding Holland Park, this area features leafy streets and some of the largest detached and semi-detached houses in London. The area also offers a good supply of flats in large mansion blocks and converted Victorian houses. It is convenient for the shopping and entertainment facilities of Kensington High Street, Notting Hill Gate and the Westfield London shopping centre. There is easy access to the West End and the City by public transport. Holland Park and Shepherd's Bush stations are easily accessible.

Maida Vale (W9)

Maida Vale has a rich supply of flats of various sizes and types. The area's wide streets are lined with large terraced houses and red-brick mansion blocks, often with access to large private gardens including some with tennis courts. The area surrounding the Grand Union Canal, known as Little Venice, has many large stucco houses, some of which remain single-family homes while others have been converted into flats.

The local tube station is Maida Vale.

Notting Hill (W11)

Just north of Kensington, Notting Hill features large houses, often with good-sized private or communal gardens, and easy access to the West End and the City by public transport. The area is close to both Holland Park and Kensington Gardens and has a large variety of local restaurants, trendy shops, bars and antique shops. Notting Hill is home to the Portobello Market and hosts the largest annual street party and carnival in Europe held over the August bank holiday weekend. Notting Hill Gate, Bayswater and Holland Park stations are all conveniently located.

North London (N and NW postcodes)

Hampstead (NW3)

Hampstead is an affluent residential community long favoured by academics, artists and media figures. The High Street is dominated by exclusive boutiques, cafes and restaurants. Its winding, hilly streets feature brick townhouses and large detached houses, many of which have been converted into flats. It is adjacent to Hampstead Heath, which has many walking paths, large ponds for swimming and fishing, art shows and city views from Parliament Hill. In the summer, there are outdoor concerts at Kenwood House, one of the most glorious country houses in London. Hampstead is serviced by both tube and overground stations including Hampstead, Hampstead Heath, Finchley Road & Frognal and Finchley Road.

Hampstead Garden Suburb (NW11)

North of Hampstead, this area is definitely a suburban enclave. It features cottages and beautiful four-, five- and six-bedroom homes as well as many stately Georgian and ambassadorial homes with well-manicured gardens. It has two small but varied shopping areas. Many homes back onto Hampstead Heath. It may be necessary to have a car.

Highgate (N6)

North-east of Hampstead Heath, Highgate Village is quietly residential with a definite country atmosphere featuring a golf club and many homes, both old and new, with large gardens. Parking and driving are quite easy. The nearby Highgate tube station is on the Northern Line.

Islington (N1)

North of the City, Islington is a friendly, lively place with modern terraced houses, Victorian villas and smartly-restored Georgian squares. Home to Camden Passage, noted for its antique shops and market, the area also enjoys easy access to the City and the West End. While there is a lack of green open spaces, the restaurants and bars along Upper Street near Angel tube station are the centre of the area's vibrant nightlife. Islington is sandwiched by two tube stations, Angel and Highbury & Islington.

Regent's Park and Primrose Hill (NW1)

The elegant residential area around Regent's Park is most famous for its Nash terraces overlooking the park. Its impressive homes include Winfield House and the residence of the US Ambassador. Modern blocks of flats, London Zoo and the Open Air Theatre all add to the diversity of the area. The more bohemian High Street of Primrose Hill offers a plethora of independent shops and restaurants as well as stunning views of London from the top of the hill. The area is serviced by Chalk Farm station.

St. John's Wood (NW8)

North-west of Regent's Park and suburban in feeling, St. John's Wood has many large detached and semi-detached houses as well as large blocks of flats with good views over the park. The American School in London is located here. St. John's Wood station is located on the Jubilee line and provides easy access to Canary Wharf and the West End. The local High

Street provides all the necessary amenities.

Swiss Cottage (NW3)

North of St. John's Wood, Swiss Cottage offers leafy streets with large blocks of flats, low terraced houses and modern townhouses with a cosmopolitan flavour. A large public leisure centre attached to the main library dominates the heart of Swiss Cottage. Swiss Cottage station is on the Jubilee Line.

The City of London and East London (EC and E postcodes)

Living in the City, London's financial centre, can provide easy access to work but it is very quiet outside of working hours. Slightly north of the City, Clerkenwell offers good transport links and a more vibrant social scene.

Relatively newly-developed areas include Shoreditch, Wapping and the Docklands. Housing is mainly either warehouses (which have been converted in the last 10 years to a very high standard) or new builds (which often have river views). Some residences have off-street parking, 24-hour porters (doormen), indoor swimming pools and other fitness facilities (these costs are often included in service charges). Transport is improving and the Docklands Light Railway runs a service between Tower Gateway, Bank, Beckton, Stratford, Greenwich and Island Gardens stations. Canary Wharf, in the heart of the Docklands, is home to a number of banks and other financial institutions, which has made East London particularly appealing to young professionals. In this up-and-coming area, new shops and restaurants continue to open regularly.

South London (SE and SW postcodes)

Battersea (SW8 and SW11)

On the south side of the Thames across from Chelsea Harbour, Battersea is dominated by Battersea Park and the recently reinvigorated Battersea Power Station. Battersea is cheaper than living north of the river and is home to many brick Victorian mansion blocks and larger late Victorian properties. With excellent facilities for shopping, parking, education, health and sports, it is very popular with young Londoners. Battersea does not have a tube station but it is served by several buses and mainline trains with fast links into Waterloo station.

Clapham (SW4 and SW9)

Always popular with families, this area surrounds Clapham Common and features large Victorian family properties on tree-lined streets with on-street parking. Clapham's three tube stations are served by the Northern line making this a recommended location for young City professionals who are looking to buy rather than rent.

Fulham (SW6)

Just west of Chelsea, Fulham has a number of large parks and is home to Chelsea Football Club. The area is popular with young English professionals and their families as well as increasing numbers of expatriates who are attracted by the larger private gardens and better value for money. The typical Fulham street is lined with two- and three-storey Victorian terraced houses, many of which have been converted into flats. Several large mansion blocks are located near the river. The local station is Fulham Broadway on the District Line.

Putney (SW15)

Along the south bank of the Thames, Putney has a chain of attractive open spaces with extensive sporting grounds, especially rowing clubs. It contains the oldest high-rise flats in London as well as many two-storey homes with gardens. There is a busy and convenient street for shopping in addition to the Putney Exchange, an enclosed shopping mall. Putney has several main line and bus links to Central London as well as a tube station (although not located particularly close to the area's residential neighbourhoods).

Shad Thames (SE1)

This riverside neighbourhood stretches east from Tower Bridge. The area boasts a high concentration of warehouse conversions and newly-constructed apartment complexes. It is also home to the Design Museum and hosts a Friday antiques sale in the nearby Bermondsey Market. There are numerous restaurants, speciality food shops, clothing stores and bookshops. Its location provides easy access to the City and the Docklands with London Bridge being the main tube stop.

Greater London

More and more newcomers to London are moving to communities farther from the centre. These communities are often less expensive and are generally regarded as good places to bring up families. Typically, the homes have larger gardens and the areas are also marked by lower crime rates and better schools. Most have every type of housing, from rows of brick terrace houses to tall stately Georgian terraces to large detached houses.

The disadvantages to these communities can be the longer commutes to central London and the City as well as the need for a car in most locations.

Barnes (SW13)

Located west of Putney on the Thames, this area features low terraced houses from the late Victorian and Edwardian eras. It has a wonderful Wetland Centre, sporting grounds and a swan pond. Barnes offers bus and train transportation.

Richmond (TW10)

South-west of Barnes, Richmond is a lovely suburban village with large houses and beautiful gardens. Home to the botanical Kew Gardens, the area also has many smaller parks which create a delightful country atmosphere. Richmond Park comprises 2,000 acres of parkland while Richmond Green is often the setting for cricket matches. Richmond station serves as both a mainline station and tube stop.

Wimbledon (SW19)

Wimbledon, famous for the tennis tournament held there every summer, is located eight miles south-west of central London. Wimbledon has a suburban atmosphere with Wimbledon Common comprising 1,200 acres of land for riders, walkers and picnickers. The village has a wide range of shopping, including the Centre Court shopping complex, and the train and tube station offers convenient transportation to London.

Other equally charming areas worth considering are

Blackheath (SE3), Dulwich (SE21), Kew (TW9), Greenwich (SE10) and Wandsworth (SW18).

Living in the countryside

Within commuting distance of London are some wonderful suburban communities with large houses and enormous gardens. There is no question that one can find almost palatial splendour in the rural areas for what one has to pay for a house in London. Yet, again, the commute into London must be considered, although trains can offer several options.

South of London, the county of Surrey encompasses many charming villages – including Cobham, Esher, Walton-on-Thames, Weybridge, West Byfleet – all with good public transport into Central London. The American School in England (TASIS), the American Community Schools (ACS) and Marymount International School are also located in Surrey.

North-west of central London are the communities of Wembley, Harrow, Pinner and Ruislip. These areas are popular for their suburban atmosphere and more garden-for-the-money value. They primarily contain semi-detached and small detached houses.

Further northwest are the communities of Northwood, Chorleywood, Moor Park and Watford – all with large houses and gardens. These areas are convenient to the London Orbital (M25) and the many suburban superstores.

DID YOU KNOW?

The term High Street refers to the main street of a neighbourhood or town. There is usually a selection of shops, restaurants, pubs and banks located on the High Street.

LETTING PROPERTY

Once you have narrowed down your list of areas, there are other crucial issues to consider depending on if you are going to rent or buy a home in London. Indeed, once you are established in London, you may see what a unique and exciting investment opportunity the city can offer.

Estate agencies located on a High Street will normally carry listings only for that particular neighbourhood. The decentralised nature of the rental market can make it difficult to look for property if you haven't narrowed your search. A good starting point is the website primelocation.com, which combines most estate agents' lists of properties to buy or rent in London and the rest of the UK (*see also Online resources* in this chapter).

The UK rental market can move quickly and properties are frequently not on the market more than one month before their availability date. As a result, it is not beneficial to house-hunt too far in advance. You may want to consider moving into temporary housing first and then taking time to find your permanent home.

Renters should be aware of the Housing Act 1988, which regulates your right to extend your tenancy and the landlord's right to repossess the property or increase the rent. Your solicitor or relocation agent can explain this in detail. You should not sign a tenancy agreement or lease without first having it approved by a solicitor familiar with such documents. Your company may have an in-house lawyer who can do this for you or you can contact the Law Society (lawsociety.org.uk) for names of firms specialising in such work.

There are two important and potentially novel aspects of the housing market that you may encounter:

1. Many rentals are fully furnished (including dishes, sheets, towels, etc.), which can make your move very straightforward. You only need to bring your clothes, the children's toys and other personal items. However, the furnishings may not be very high quality. It may be possible to negotiate with the owner to remove the furnishings and move in your own, though the owner may ask you to pay for the storage costs. If you find you need additional storage for furniture that will not fit into your house or flat, you will need to research the best options for

you based on location, size of storage unit, price point etc. A good starting point is <u>whatstorage.co.uk</u> where you can compare self-storage unit prices in your location.

2. Some rentals are only available as a 'company let', which means that the lease is made out to your corporation and must be signed by the Managing Director or his or her appointee. The company therefore guarantees the tenancy.

Defining your rental checklist

For happy renting, it is important to get the legal and practical aspects right. Negotiation is all about striking a balance between your needs and requirements and those of the landlord. Here are a few tips:

Read the small print

A tenancy agreement is a document that sets out the terms of a tenancy and there are various types of tenancy agreements:

- assured shorthold tenancy (AST)
- excluded tenancy (lodging)
- assured tenancy
- non-assured tenancy
- regulated tenancy
- company let

The most common form of tenancy is the assured shorthold tenancy (AST). When reviewing your tenancy agreement, you should watch out for the following:

- Do you have a break clause? Job mobility makes it sensible to be able to terminate early and this is usually granted subject to a minimum tenure of six months. Read the language carefully regarding the notice period to see if the lease permits termination at six months or permits you to give notice of termination at six months. In the latter case, termination will occur at seven or eight months depending on the required notice period.

- Do you have an option to renew? You may want an option to extend for a second or third year.

- What is the level of annual rent increase? It is likely to be no less than the Retail Price Index (i.e., inflation) but a minimum of either 3 per cent or 5 per cent. A maximum percentage can also be negotiated.

Be prepared

- Rent is expressed on a per week basis. As there are 52 weeks in a year, your monthly rent is equivalent to 4.3 weeks – not four weeks.

- As of 1st June 2019, landlords are only be able to take five weeks' rent as a tenancy deposit. This increases to six weeks for properties whose rent exceeds £50,000 per year. The deposit may not be returned until you have proved that you have settled your utility bills.

- If you are asked for a holding deposit to secure a tenancy, make sure it is refundable against the full deposit.

- Sort out your wish list at the negotiation stage (e.g. redecoration, linens or a microwave). It is difficult to go back to the landlord later.

- There may be additional charges for related matters such as drawing up tenancy agreements and check-ins.

Best practice

- Set up a Standing Order Mandate (direct debit) to pay the rent. You are obliged to pay on time.

- You have no legal right to withhold rent, whatever your grievance, so discuss any problems with your agent.

- Ensure your check-in is conducted by an independent inventory clerk as this will form the basis of the dilapidation charges. Take photographs of any existing damages, no matter how minor, and keep them with your copy of the inventory check.

- Take care with picture hooks or you may end up redecorating. Review the terms of your tenancy agreement to make sure you are complying with any specific requirements.

- Make sure the utilities (e.g. gas, water, electricity, telephone, television licence and council tax) are transferred into your name at the onset and out of your name when you leave.

- Get to know your managing agents and be realistic about what they can achieve – that way you will get the best out of them. It is rare in the UK for a tenant to talk directly to the landlord during negotiations. The normal process is for the tenant to talk to his or her agent, who then talks with the landlord's agent, who then talks with the landlord.

- Protect your belongings with tenants' contents insurance. Normally, the landlord insures the property and its contents (if furnished) and the tenant is responsible for his or her own belongings. Insurance quotes can be lower if certain security devices such as locks and security alarms are installed. If possible, obtain an insurance quote before finalising the tenancy agreement so that you can request that the landlord install the proper devices. To find an insurance broker the website of British Insurance Brokers Association (biba.org.uk) is a good starting place.

- Always get your property professionally cleaned when you leave. Domestic cleaning is no substitute. Ensure that your tenancy agreement includes the requirement that the property be professionally cleaned before you move in.

- There are now Tenancy Deposit Protection schemes in place for many rental properties to ensure your deposit is kept safe. Insist on your deposit being held in such a scheme. For more information, including advice on resolving disputes, visit: gov.uk (search *Housing and local services*).

Know your neighbourhood

- Proximity to schools/parks/playgrounds.

- Proximity to amenities (shops, restaurants and pubs).

- Is there a local supermarket?

- Proximity to the bus, tube and/or train – is there an easy link to work?

- Availability of on-street or off-street parking.

- Level of crime in the area – check with local police if necessary.

Household tips

Look for:

- Storage space and bedroom wardrobe space.

- Electrical points for appliances, PC, TV & video, stereo, etc.

- Burglar and smoke alarms.

- Separate washing machine and dryer (they are often combined). If you do a lot of laundry and have a combination machine, you may want to ask your landlord to install a separate dryer if space permits.

- Refrigerator/freezer size (UK appliances are often smaller).

- Shower pressure (power showers).

- Access – are there too many stairs? Are the common areas of a good standard?

- Height and width of the corridors and stairwells (especially in conversions) for moving furniture in and out.

- Outside space – do you have access to the garden or will you have to share? Who is responsible for maintenance?

COUNCIL TAX

Council tax is a local tax set by each local council to help pay for local services such as rubbish collection and street cleaning. There will be one bill per dwelling to be paid by the resident (or by the owner where the property is untenanted). The amount paid will be based on the value of the dwelling.

DID YOU KNOW?

Single occupants receive a 25 per cent discount on council tax. Full-time students do not have to pay council tax, but must apply for an exemption from the council.

BUYING PROPERTY

For those not familiar with buying property in London, the experience can be daunting, distressing, time consuming and expensive. But if you are planning on being in London longer term, it can definitely be a worthwhile investment. It will pay dividends to acquaint yourself with basic procedures and terms and to obtain good professional advice. One of the most common reasons that property sales in the UK fail is that no deposits are required until contracts are exchanged; the buyer is under no legal obligation to buy the property, the seller is under no legal obligation to sell and neither the buyer nor the seller have to compensate the other for any of the costs that the other party may have incurred.

Acquisition costs

Finder's fee

This is the fee paid to a property search or purchase management company for representing you (the buyer) and finding your property. You do not have to pay this fee if you register with a normal estate agent and/or reply to an advertisement for a property. Remember that an estate agent represents the seller's interest – not yours.

Land Registry fees

This is the cost of registering the buyer as the new owner at the Land Registry (landregistry.gov.uk).

Legal fees

This includes the solicitor's fee for acting on your behalf in the purchase. The fee can vary quite significantly so it is advisable to obtain a quote from several solicitors before proceeding.

Lender's arrangement fee

Lenders may charge you for organising your mortgage. This may be a flat fee or a percentage of the total advance. They may also require legal representation using a solicitor from their designated panel. Some lenders will make a contribution towards legal fees.

Local searches

These are searches undertaken by your solicitor with the local council to ensure that there are no apparent reasons for not proceeding with the purchase. The searches take about four weeks and cost approximately £300.

Stamp duty

This is a government tax levied on the purchase price of a property. If the purchase price is below a certain threshold, you don't pay any stamp duty. If it is above the threshold, you pay between 1 and 4 percent of the entire purchase price on a sliding scale. For further details, visit the HM Revenue & Customs website: gov.uk/government/organisations/hm-revenue-customs.

Survey fees

This covers the cost of the survey conducted to determine that the property has no significant structural faults. The lenders may insist on a particular type of survey but they may make a contribution towards the cost of it.

Conveyancing (legal) process

Estate agent(s)

These are the selling agents, who receive a fee from the seller to achieve a sale at the best possible price.

Formulating the offer

Your bid will be given to the estate agent, who will forward it to the seller for acceptance. Your ability to negotiate will depend on the current market. If you offer the asking price, you should ask for a period of exclusivity (when another contract cannot be issued). However, it should be noted that this is not legally binding.

Exchange of contracts

At this stage, which takes place approximately one month after the initial offer providing you have received your mortgage offer, you will enter into a legally binding contract with the seller, who can no longer accept other offers. You will normally pay a 10 per cent deposit.

Completion

This usually occurs within one to four weeks after the exchange of contracts, at which time you become the legal owner of the property and obtain possession.

Gazumping

This is when the seller agrees a price with the buyer and then sells to another buyer for a higher price.

Gazundering

This is when the buyer drives down the agreed price

by threatening to pull out of the agreed purchase just before exchange of contracts.

Insurance

If you are buying a house, you are responsible for building insurance from the exchange of contracts. With flats, you pay for this via the service charge. You will require contents insurance at completion to cover your belongings.

Mortgages

This is the term for a housing loan, normally up to 70 to 80 percent of the purchase price and for a period up to 30 years.

Capital repayment

In this type of mortgage, the instalment payment covers interest as well as repaying the capital borrowed.

Endowment

This mortgage uses the maturity value of an endowment policy to pay off the borrowing at the end of the term. Be aware that at maturity, the assurance policy may not cover the full loan sum.

Interest only

This type of mortgage payment only covers the interest that is accumulating on the loan. In this case it is advisable to have collateral security to pay off the capital at the end of the term.

SURVEYS

Homebuyer's report and valuation

This is normally used by the homebuyer to obtain basic structural information.

Full structural survey

This is a more expensive but comprehensive report highlighting significant faults, which may lead to further negotiation of the property purchase price.

Mortgage valuation

This is a visual inspection carried out by the bank to confirm the property valuation.

TYPES OF PROPERTY CHARGES

Ground rent

This is the sum paid to the owner of the freehold for use of the land over which your property is built.

Service charge

This is the flat owner's annual contribution to the running costs of a building (e.g. porter, lift, lighting, cleaning).

Sinking fund

This is a reserve fund collected annually to provide for major works (e.g. external redecoration).

TYPES OF TENURE

Freehold

This is the outright purchase of a building, normally a house, and land 'in perpetuity'.

Leasehold

The purchase of a right to occupy a house or, more normally, a flat, for a specified number of years, up to

999 years. The land and main structure of the property is owned by the freeholder, who charges ground rent. Leases confer obligations on the lessee and the landlord. Property values diminish as leases shorten but owner-occupiers have a statutory right, subject to certain terms, to extend their lease for a further 90 years. For purposes of making a sound investment, it is typically recommended to obtain a property with at least 80 years on the leasehold.

Share of freehold

In some cases, the building lessees combine together to buy the freehold. A management company is normally set up to purchase it and the lessees take a share. Among other benefits, it is then possible to extend the lease term without the payment of a premium.

Online resources

- Zoopla: zoopla.co.uk
    - Search a postcode or area to determine historical value.
- Money Supermarket: moneysupermarket.com
    - Excellent mortgage search engine.
- Mouse Price: mouseprice.com
    - Search by postcode to receive a local guide of an area or free valuation of a home or flat.
- Nestoria: nestoria.co.uk

o Search engines for properties to sell and rent.

- Our Property: ourproperty.co.uk

  o Free house price information from Land Registry databases.

- Primelocation: primelocation.com

  o A property portal that lists up-market properties in the UK and abroad. It accepts property listings only from estate agents, letting agents and new home developers.

- Right Move: rightmove.co.uk

  o Search engine for properties to sell and rent.

BRITISH REAL ESTATE TERMINOLOGY

The following list of real estate terminology will hopefully eliminate any confusion in communication and help you interpret your property's particulars.

A home by any other name

There is a host of different descriptions for property, especially in London. Here are a few of the most common:

- Bedsit: Single room, rented accommodation combining bedroom and sitting room with a shared bathroom.

- Bungalow: One-level ground-floor house, very rare in central London.

- Conversion: A flat in a house that was originally built for single-family occupancy.

- Cottage: Small rustic-style house, generally old, often with a garden.

- Detached house: A house that stands apart from any others, generally surrounded by its own garden.

- Edwardian: Period property built between 1901 and 1910.

- Flat: An apartment, usually on one floor, that may be in a block or in a large converted house.

- Georgian: Period property built between 1714 and 1830.

- Maisonette: An apartment arranged over two or more floors, usually with its own separate entrance.

- Mansion block: Period apartment building, often Victorian, Edwardian or Art Deco, built specifically to provide flats.

- Mansion flat: Large, traditionally old-fashioned apartment, usually in a good area. Often possessing large rooms, good storage space and lacking modern conveniences until refurbished.

- Mews house: Converted carriage house with smaller rooms and lower ceilings than a typical period house, lots of character and often with garage.

- New build: A new development of flats or houses.

- Period property: A property built before 1911 and named after the period in which it was built.

- Purpose-built block: A modern building of flats built specifically for this purpose.

- Semi-detached house: A house that is joined to another house on only one side, often with its own garden.

- Studio flat: A one-room flat with a separate bathroom and kitchen or kitchenette.

- Terraced house: One of a row of similar houses joined together, mainly built in Victorian times.

- Townhouse Typical: Central London home, often located in a Georgian or Victorian terrace, usually two to five storeys high.

- Victorian: Period property built between 1837 to 1901.

The ABCs of property

Know your abbreviations. These are some of the most commonly used.

- CH: Central heating.

- CHW: Constant hot water.

- F/F: Fully furnished. Equipped with furniture, soft furnishings and accessories for immediate occupation.

- GFCH or GCH: Gas-fired central heating (as opposed to oil-fired).

- OSP: Off-street parking, which is free and unrestricted.

- Respark: Residents' parking. Council-approved on-street parking. Usually unrestricted access in allocated areas for two vehicles per household for a small annual fee.

- U/F: Unfurnished. No furniture but generally with carpets, light fixtures and appliances.

- WC: Literally 'water closet', but really a room with toilet and wash basin.

Chapter 3:

Money, banking and taxation

When moving to London, one of the first tasks you will find yourself confronted with (after sorting out the different pound notes and coins) is opening a UK bank account. When choosing a bank, consider the services you will need – direct deposit, bill payment, international transfers, credit cards or different currency accounts. As an international centre of finance with hundreds of thousands employed in the industry, London offers a wealth of information. As you organise your finances, remember to consider tax implications and consult an expert where necessary.

BRITISH CURRENCY

British currency, often referred to as sterling, is comprised of two monetary units – the pence and the pound. One pound equals 100 pence. Coins include the 1 pence, 2 pence, 5 pence, 10 pence, 20 pence, 50 pence, the 1 pound coin and the 2 pound coin. The bills are called pound notes and come in denominations of 5, 10, 20 and 50 pound notes. There are no paper versions of the 1 and 2 pound coins. Pence are commonly abbreviated as p (e.g. 10p), and the pound sign is £ (e.g. £10) while the currency code is GBP. You may also hear a pound called a quid. (e.g. that will be five quid (£5)).

DID YOU KNOW?

The term 'quid' comes from the Latin expression 'quid pro quo' meaning one thing in return for another, no doubt dating back to the Roman occupation of Britain.

UK BANKING

Many of your banking needs will likely be determined by your main source of income. If you are moving to the UK as an expatriate, your company may choose to continue to pay your salary in your local currency and provide an adjustment for the difference in the cost of living. If this is the case, please speak with a financial adviser prior to moving to London and look into options regarding opening an offshore banking account for tax implications.

It is generally a good idea to open a local currency account with a UK bank. The major banks offer essentially the same services (and can provide accounts that hold multiple currencies). Therefore, you will probably choose the bank with which your company has a business relationship or the bank located nearest to your home or office.

Some of the largest UK and international banks, with branches throughout London and the UK, are:

- Barclays Bank: barclays.co.uk
- Citibank: citibank.co.uk
- Coutts: coutts.com
- HSBC: hsbc.co.uk
- Lloyds Bank: lloydsbank.com
- National Westminster Bank (Natwest): personal.natwest.com
- Royal Bank of Scotland: rbs.co.uk
- First Direct: firstdirect.com

Digital/internet-only banks

Banks in the UK are acutely aware of the risk of fraud and money laundering and take several measures to prevent such crimes, which are particularly noticeable to people opening accounts. Sometimes it can take up to six weeks to open an account or to clear international cheques so be sure to have alternative sources for accessing money on arrival.

The verification of the identity of new customers may be a rigorous process, including requiring original identity documents (i.e. passport, identity card and/or utility bills) or certified copies of the same. A letter of introduction from your employer may be required as well as proof of address in the UK. If you require immediate credit facilities, copies of your previous country's bank statements or a letter of introduction from your previous bank will also help to speed the process.

Banking services

UK banks offer two basic types of accounts – current (chequing) accounts and deposit (savings) accounts – although there are variations of each type. Building societies (similar to the US savings and loans associations) also offer current accounts. Most British banks now offer interest on select current accounts and will provide free banking for personal customers who remain in good credit standing. Some banks will also provide sweep accounts. This means that the bank will automatically transfer excess funds from your current account to your deposit account. Conversely, the bank will move funds from your deposit account to your current account to maintain the agreed credit balance. You should obtain a direct debit/cheque guarantee card for your current account (see Cheques and debit cards in this chapter). At the request of the customer, statements are sent quarterly or monthly. Cancelled cheques are returned only if requested and a fee is frequently charged.

Monthly or quarterly bills (e.g. telephone, electricity, gas, water and council tax) may be paid at your bank by three methods. One method is to use the giro slips attached to most bills. The giro slips can be grouped together and all paid with a single cheque. The bank stamps your bill to provide a record of payment, proving beneficial as cheques are not normally returned by the bank. The second method is paying electronically online each month or quarter. The third method of payment is the use of standing orders or direct debit. With a standing order, you instruct your bank to pay a fixed amount to a specific payee at regular intervals, usually on a certain day each month (e.g. £1,000 rent on the 15th of every month to the landlord or estate agent). With a direct debit, you authorise your bank to pay on demand varying amounts as specified by a particular supplier (e.g. whatever the electricity company states is your monthly or quarterly bill). For additional information on paying utilities, see Chapter 5: Utilities.

Bank hours

Regular banking hours are 9:00-17:00 or 9:30-16:30, Monday to Friday. Many bank branches stay open late once per week (until 17:30 or 18:00) as well as being open on Saturdays (9:00-9:30 until 12:30 or 15:30). All banks are closed on holidays (hence the term Bank Holiday). Many banks close by 12:00 or 14:00 on Christmas Eve and do not reopen until after Boxing Day. All major banks have 24-hour cash machines (ATM).

DID YOU KNOW?

You can ask for cashback when paying for your items with a debit card at UK supermarkets and often at local shops such as pharmacies. Cashback is usually not charged and is handy if you need cash without having to go to a cash machine. Cash machines in the UK do not accept deposits except at certain terminals inside the bank branch.

Cheques and debit cards

Writing a sterling cheque may differ slightly from writing cheques elsewhere. When drafting a cheque there are two important points to remember:

1. The date is written with the day, the month and then the year (e.g. 5th March 2018 or 5-3-18). Do remember either to put the day first or spell out the month.

2. To write the amount, you must write 'pounds' and 'p' or 'pence'. For example, £10.62 is written: 'Ten

pounds and 62p' or 'Ten pounds and sixty-two pence'.

Sterling cheques are usually crossed, meaning they have two vertical lines running down the middle. A crossed cheque is for deposit only and cannot be cashed by a third party. Hence, cheques are not endorsed for cash in the UK. All UK banks are now on a three-to-five-day clearing cycle at the bank's discretion. Most banks, however, credit cash deposits immediately.

Importantly, in addition to any credit cards you may apply for, you should obtain a direct debit/cheque guarantee card for your current account. Well-known versions of the direct debit card are Maestro and Visa. This card will let you pay for goods and services wherever you see the Maestro or Visa logo and gives you access to your money from cash machines across the UK as well as guaranteeing your cheque up to the amount shown on the card. Although you may cash a cheque for any amount at your own bank branch (where you opened the account), you will be required to show your cheque card when cashing a cheque at either another branch of your bank or at another chain of banks. If the cheque amount is over the limit stated on your card, you will often need to make prior arrangements even within your own branch in order to cash it.

Whenever you use your direct debit/cheque guarantee card, the transactions will appear on your account statement, which will provide you with a clear audit trail of your transactions. Purchases are limited, however, to available funds (or an agreed overdraft).

DID YOU KNOW?

Most establishments in the UK have adopted contactless payment for purchases up to £30. For purchases of a greater amount, you must use Chip and PIN as a more secure way to pay with credit or debit cards. Instead of using your signature to verify payments, you must enter a four-digit Personal Identification Number (PIN) known only to you. If you do not know your PIN, you will be asked to use an alternative method of payment.

Credit cards

Most major banks issue credit cards in the form of a Visa or MasterCard, which can be used throughout the UK and in Europe where the appropriate sign is displayed. Similar cards from other countries are also accepted.

Obtaining a UK credit card can be difficult initially if you do not already have a credit history in the UK. A letter or phone call from your company can help speed up the process. American Express also offers credit cards in the UK. If you hold an American Express card in your home country, they may be able to assist you in transferring your card to the UK. Please keep in mind that many establishments in the UK do not accept American Express cards so it is helpful to also own a Visa or MasterCard or debit card. In addition, many services in the UK charge you a fee when you use a credit card.

Traveller's cheques

Traveller's cheques and foreign currency can be purchased from all major UK banks. However, it is usually necessary to give a few days' notice and order ahead. Importantly, foreign currency can also be ordered at most UK Post Office branches (but often not at the postal counters that can be found in retail stores like your local chemist or newsstand).

Transferring money

If you want to transfer money from your previous home country to your UK current account, you can have it sent by wire transfer (SWIFT) with the help of your previous banker or a transfer by TELEX can be completed in 48 hours. An online banking service is also a fast and potentially cheaper alternative as they move money internationally at the real exchange rate (the rate you'll find on independent sources such as Google, XE and Yahoo Finance.)

Alternatively, you can purchase sterling from your UK bank with a foreign currency cheque (e.g. in dollars drawn from your home country bank account). The time it takes for the foreign cheque to clear and be credited to your UK account will vary by type of currency and the size of the cheque and, in some cases, may take several weeks. If timing is important, be sure to check with your bank before you proceed.

If you wish to remit money to another foreign country, you can ask your UK bank to draw a draft on your behalf against the sterling in your current account or to transfer the amount to a foreign bank account.

Additionally, there are now many online firms specialising in foreign money transfers, often for a much-reduced fee compared to high street banks. PayPal, amongst others, can be a more economical way to transfer smaller sums of money to friends or relatives.

DID YOU KNOW?

As an expatriate living in the UK, you pay UK taxes on any money you bring into the country, especially if it comes from an interest-bearing account. It is advised to open an offshore account and transfer funds prior to moving to the UK. Speak with a financial or tax adviser for more tips.

Safe deposit boxes

Although local commercial banks often provide 'strong rooms' for storing their customers' valuables, they do not have facilities for individual safety deposit boxes. Privately-run safe deposit centres offer these boxes instead. Metropolitan Safe Deposits is one of the UK's leading independent safe deposit companies. There are two locations in London: Knightsbridge and St. John's Wood. Visit the website metrosafe.co.uk for more details.

TAXATION

When you come to reside in the UK, your tax status changes and HMRC has primary jurisdiction over your income (hmrc.gov.uk). Depending on your home nation, you may have a tax obligation to your 'home' country and may be required to report and pay income tax there as well. This is true for American citizens, who can refer to the section on American taxes in this chapter. In almost all cases, however, you will want to consult a tax advisor soon after you arrive regarding your tax status and filing requirements.

UK taxes

The UK tax year runs from the 6th of April to the 5th of April the following year. If you send in a paper tax return, it must reach HMRC by midnight on the 31st of October. If you file your tax return online, it must reach HMRC by midnight on the 31st of January. There is no exception if the filing deadline falls on a weekend or public holiday. Interest and penalties may be charged on tax not paid by the due date and penalties will be levied for tax returns filed late.

If you are employed by a firm in the UK, the tax on your earnings will be calculated and withheld at source via the PAYE (Pay As You Earn) system. It is prudent from time to time to make sure that the correct level of tax is being withheld, especially at the start of a new employment or a new tax year. If you are self-employed, your accountant can advise you on how to make estimated payments or you may consult with your nearest HMRC office. In addition to wages, you will be taxed on any investment income that is sourced in the UK, along with any income from your investments outside the UK that is remitted to the UK. Please consult the HMRC website for further information:

(gov.uk/government/organisations/hm-revenue-customs)

National Insurance (similar to the United States Social Security) in the UK is payable through withholding if you are an employee and payable with your income tax return or by direct debit if you are self-employed. If you are an American working in the UK, you will be required to pay either Social Security tax to the United States (US) or National Insurance tax to the UK but not both. The length of your anticipated stay in the UK should determine which plan to pay. Generally, you must have a US employer to be eligible to pay US FICA whilst resident in the UK.

Finally, VAT (Value Added Tax) is a tax that you pay as a consumer when purchasing goods and services. In the UK, the standard rate is currently 20 per cent (from January 2011). Some services, like domestic energy, are charged at a reduced rate of 5 percent. You do not pay VAT on items considered to be 'essentials' such as newspapers, children's clothing and most groceries.

American taxes

American citizens are taxed by the US government on their worldwide income but are given a tax credit, subject to limitations, for foreign income taxes paid. In general, American citizens, wherever they live in the world, must file a tax return if their income exceeds a certain amount.

Further information is available from the IRS for US citizens residing abroad either from the IRS office of the US Embassy: irs.gov

However, US taxpayers living in the UK are potentially entitled to sizeable exclusions/deductions on their foreign earned income if they meet certain criteria. Please consult the IRS website or office for further information.

Tax assistance

For further information on your UK or US tax obligations, you may contact HMRC, the IRS, your UK or US accountant /lawyer or your company's personnel or expatriate employee departments. For UK tax enquiries, there are various local enquiry offices in London which you can find on the HMRC website (hmrc.gov.uk). The IRS office in the US Embassy can assist you, at no cost, in filing your US returns and the Consular Office of the US Embassy (uk.usembassy.gov) has lists of American accountants and lawyers who can assist you for a fee.

There are a few small UK firms who specialise in US

expatriates residing in the UK. These include:

- Buzzacott LLP: buzzacott.co.uk
- MacIntyre Hudson: macintyrehudson.co.uk

Canadian taxes

In general, if you can establish that you are no longer a resident of Canada, you do not have to pay taxes in Canada on income earned outside Canada. Specific questions can be directed to the International Tax Services Office. Information may also be accessed on the Canada Revenue Agency website: canada.ca.en/services/taxes.

Chapter 4:

Working in

London

Any job search, regardless of location, requires persistence and tenacity. There are aspects of working in the UK which differ from that of working in other countries. Within London, roles based in financial services, law and even the charity sector are often filled via recruitment firms. Your legal standing in the UK regarding your entitlement to work is especially important and it is essential that you understand your legal entitlement to work.

THE JOB SEARCH

If you have arrived in London as a result of a partner's relocation and need to seek employment, job hunting may prove to be a creative task that can require considerable initiative. It is frequently claimed that only 80% of job openings are advertised. Recruiters and employment consultants will tell you that the best way to find a job is through networking.

In addition to any connections you may have made through referrals from your home country as well as former employers and friends, below is a list of some resources that can help you to start your job search in London.

FOCUS Information Services

FOCUS is a not-for-profit organisation, staffed entirely by expatriates, that provides its members with, among other services, programmes on working in the UK. FOCUS operates a comprehensive Career Development Programme designed for the various stages of a career search.

FOCUS resources include several publications to aid the expatriate in getting started in the UK. Topics include British curriculum vitae (CV or résumé) preparation, job websites, resource lists, networking groups and tips, interviewing strategies and much more. Additional resources for job seekers are available on their website: focus-info.org.

Recruitment consultants

The Executive Grapevine: The UK Directory of Recruitment Consultants can be a good starting point for further information regarding recruiters. Here you will find an online directory of recruitment consultants in a wide variety of businesses (executivegrapevine.com).

The distinctions between different types of recruitment firms may not always be clear. Recruitment consultants often work in at least one of the following ways:

Executive search

Executive search firms (often referred to as "head hunters") are retained by a corporate client on a fee basis to find an appropriate candidate to fill a particular role. This type of search is typically for senior-level positions for which the pool of suitable candidates is relatively small. Executive search firms target the best candidates for a position, whether or not they are actively looking for a new job.

Advertised selection

Recruitment firms are retained by a corporate client to advertise in order to find candidates for a specific role.

This approach relies on job candidates actively searching to find job listings of interest. Typically, the recruitment firm will review all CVs and cover letters received and then interview the most relevant candidates. A shortlist of interviewed candidates is then presented to the client for the next stage of the interview process. Advertised selection is most frequently used for hiring middle management positions.

Contingent recruitment

Fees charged to a corporate client by a contingent recruitment firm are conditional on a job placement being made. This type of recruitment relies on job seekers registering their CV with the recruitment firm or responding to an advertised position. Corporate clients will usually select more than one contingent recruitment firm for a particular search in order to identify the most desirable pool of candidates. This type of recruitment is most common with lower salary bands as well as with temporary and contract positions.

Contingent recruitment is also used for more senior roles in markets where there are many suitable candidates. It is important to understand how the firm will use any personal information that you provide. Make sure your personal details are not passed on to a potential employer without your approval.

Networking

Networking is a key aspect of the job search. Many jobs are never advertised and are filled by word of mouth and personal recommendation. Friends, relatives, former employers and colleagues, members of professional organisations and neighbours are all potential networking contacts.

Alumni associations and clubs in London can be good sources for networking. There are also numerous networking groups in the UK that welcome newcomers. The FOCUS Resource Centre maintains an extensive list of networking organisations for members.

Additionally, LinkedIn.com is increasingly essential to a successful job search. Be sure to have an active presence on LinkedIn and keep your profile up-to-date.

Maintaining a good network is demanding and needs ongoing maintenance and development. Acquaintances that do not have employment information today may have some tomorrow.

Key networking tips include:

- Keep records of all networking contacts in one place.

- Keep in touch with networking contacts regularly but not obtrusively.

- Be a good networker for others – the benefits should go both ways.

- Try to ask at the end of networking efforts whether the individual knows of anyone who may be able to assist in your job search.

Volunteering

Volunteering can be a temporary or long-term alternative to full-time paid employment. Volunteering offers a great way to build your CV while you look for paid employment as well as offering another source of networking contacts. The following organisations can help you identify a volunteer position for your needs and interests:

- Do-it: do-it.org

  o National database of volunteering opportunities in the UK. Can advise on local volunteer bureau.

- Junior League of London: jll.org.uk

  o An organisation of women volunteers committed to promoting voluntary service, developing the potential of women and improving the London community.

- REACH: reachvolunteering.org.uk

  o Enables voluntary organisations to benefit from business, managerial, technical and professional expertise of people offering relevant career skills.

- TimeBank: timebank.org.uk

WORKING IN THE UK

Working regulations for non-UK nationals are complex and subject to change at any time. It is recommended that you undertake professional advice regarding your specific situation and eligibility to work in the UK. The UK Home Office is a good source of initial information with interactive tools to assist you in determining your eligibility for various visa categories on their website: gov.uk (search *Visas and Immigration*).

Employment rights

UK employers provide a statement of employment or contract to the employee that clearly indicates the following information:

- Names of the employer and employee.
- Job title or a brief job description.
- Where the employee is expected to work.
- Date the employment started (or is set to start).
- Details of salary and when payment will be made (e.g. weekly or monthly).
- Hours of work and any related issues such as overtime. An employee may be expected to work beyond the contractual hours for no additional pay if more work is required.
- Holiday entitlement (most UK workers receive 20-25 days per year).

- Sick pay entitlement and procedures.

- Notice of termination period – standard notice is one month but this can vary between industries and positions within a company.

- Pension scheme details.

- Length of the contract if the employee is working for a fixed time period.

- Details of the existence of any relevant collective agreements that directly affect the terms and conditions of employment, including Maternity Leave provision.

More information on employment rights is available through: gov.uk.

National Insurance numbers

National Insurance (NI) numbers are assigned to individuals who reside in the UK for use when dealing with the Inland Revenue and the Department of Work and Pensions. The NI number ensures correct credit and a record of National Insurance benefits. Employers use the number for deducting taxes and National Insurance contributions from employees' pay.

When working in the UK, it is necessary to obtain an NI number. Contact a Department for Work and Pensions office and make an appointment to be interviewed for the NI number. It is necessary to complete an application form and submit evidence of identity at the interview.

More information can be obtained from the Department for Work and Pensions: dwp.gov.uk.

Chapter 5:

Utilities

Upon moving to London, one of the first tasks will be to set up all of your utility accounts from paying council tax, gas, water and electric bills, to getting the internet, a telephone line and digital television installed. Often your letting or estate agent can help you with contacting various utilities.

With the exception of water, consumers in the London area have a variety of utility suppliers. For electricity and gas, a wide range of services and price structures are available. Moreover, switching from one supplier to another is relatively easy. To compare major utility prices and services in your area, visit the following websites:

- Unravelit: <u>unravelit.com</u>

- uSwitch: <u>uswitch.com</u>

- Money Super Market: <u>moneysupermarket.com</u>

- Broadband TV-Phone: <u>broadband-tv-phone.co</u>

LOCAL COUNCILS

Each council works to meet the needs of residents and to provide various community services including:

- operating state-funded schools
- maintaining roads and pavements
- ensuring rubbish is promptly collected

Whether you are renting or own your property, you are responsible for paying the council tax, which covers these services. Below are the local council contact details for central London:

- London Borough of Camden: <u>camden.gov.uk</u>
- Corporation of London: <u>cityoflondon.gov.uk</u>
- London Borough of Hackney: <u>hackney.gov.uk</u>
- London Borough of Hammersmith and Fulham: <u>lbhf.gov.uk</u>
- London Borough of Islington: <u>islington.gov.uk</u>
- Royal Borough of Kensington & Chelsea: <u>rbkc.gov.uk</u>
- London Borough of Lambeth: <u>lambeth.gov.uk</u>
- London Borough of Southwark: <u>southwark.gov.uk</u>
- Westminster City Council: <u>westminster.gov.uk</u>

- London Borough of Wandsworth:
  <u>wandsworth.gov.uk</u>

TELEPHONE

Public phone boxes

London's red telephone boxes are iconic and luckily, there are still a few of them around. On the whole, however, public telephones are increasingly a thing of the past and difficult to find outside the more tourist friendly areas (mainly for iconic photo opportunities). Generally, everyone has a mobile phone.

Mobile telephones

Common mobile providers include O2, Three, EE and Vodafone. Most of these companies offer services that will work throughout Continental Europe and potentially the US. To help decide on the right provider and plan, consider how often and where you will use your mobile phone (UK, Europe or the rest of the world), how long you want your service contract to last and the ease of ending the contract.

Many mobile providers have stand-alone shops on most high streets and throughout London. If you change providers, it is usually possible to keep your mobile number. However, this is based on agreements between mobile phone companies. You do not have a legal right to keep the same number.

The month-to-month contracts can offer more flexibility and cost less but usually offer fewer incentives and extras. Often, with these contracts, you must also purchase the phone outright or have an unlocked phone.

Similarly, pay-as-you-go contracts can be an economical option but be aware of your data allowance and the potential to run out of credit at inconvenient moments. However, access may be easier for customers without a local credit history.

Of greatest importance will likely be the data allowance available to you and whether or not you will be using your mobile phone to call overseas. Most mobile phone providers now offer very preferential rates for overseas calling so be sure to ask. Also be sure to find out if you can change your data plan should you need more or less – there are many free Wi-Fi spots in London, but often it is easier to use the mobile network for quick browsing and checking email.

Also consider if you are likely to use applications such as WhatsApp, Facetime, iMessage and Skype to communicate with friends and family overseas rather than text messages and phone calls as again, this can dramatically impact your data plan.

Landlines

It is becoming increasingly common in the UK for people to go without a landline. Be aware, however, that certain services may charge a premium for access via a mobile. Landline providers include:

- BT (British Telecom): <u>bt.com</u>
- Virgin Media: <u>virginmedia.com</u>
- TalkTalk: <u>talktalk.co.uk</u>

For help and advice on telephone companies and services, the UK's independent regulator and competition authority for the UK communications industries, Ofcom, has a useful website: <u>ofcom.org.uk</u>.

It is fairly easy to switch phone companies. In the UK, if you change your phone line and remain at the same address, you can keep your phone number. However, phone companies may make a reasonable charge for this service.

Before making any final decision, it is recommended that you check with the individual telephone companies for their latest prices. Bundling telephone services with additional services such as broadband and TV subscription services might enable you to take advantage of any special discounts from the provider. A little research can go a long way as the packages and costs differ across providers. It is also recommended that you check on the quality of service offered in your local area by a particular provider as this can vary by location.

Calculating the cost of various phone services can be complicated because you need to consider:

- line rental
- cost of calls
- discount packages
- number of calls you make and when
- type of calls you mostly make (local, national, international or internet)

Currently most calls, including local calls, are charged on a per-minute and per-unit basis. Telephone charges are based on metered units. The unit charge varies according to the time the call is made for local, national and international calls. Calls tend to be less expensive between 18:00 and 08:00. Some free numbers include those with prefixes of 0800, 0808 or 0321.

Numbers with the prefix 0345 or 0845 are charged at local rates. Numbers with the prefix 0900 or 0870 are charged at the national rate even if you make a local call.

New telephone equipment is available at online BT (British Telecom) shops, any high street electronics retailer or at online retailers such as Currys (currys.co.uk) or Argos (argos.co.uk). New telephone equipment can also be rented from several of the telephone service suppliers, including BT. You can also purchase a phone adapter that will enable you to use a foreign telephone in the UK.

Telephone directories, including Yellow Pages, are published for London and all other cities and towns in the UK. The dialling codes for UK cities and towns are listed in the front of each directory.

If you need flexibility, be careful when selecting a telephone contract as some may have inflexible terms and you may be liable for payments until the end of the contract period.

INTERNET

Broadband and wireless options are plentiful and roughly the same price for similar quality of service.

Broadband (cable/ASDL) service is fast. In the UK, broadband is often tied to your home phone line – so you will need to have a home phone line. This is most easily done by choosing a bundled service from the likes of British Telecom, Virgin Media, Sky or TalkTalk.

Wireless (Wi-Fi) Internet allows you to access the Internet anywhere in your house or, if provided by mobile operators, anywhere within the coverage area. This is particularly useful if you have more than one home computer or tablet. Some providers may supply a wireless router with your service. Some of the common Internet providers include:

- BT (British Telecom): bt.com
- Virgin Media: virginmedia.com
- TalkTalk: talktalk.co.uk
- Sky: sky.com

TELEVISION

All users of television sets must possess an annual TV licence, obtainable from any Post Office or through TV Licensing at tvlicensing.co.uk. One licence, which is valid for 12 months, covers all of the television sets in a household. Fines for not having a TV licence can be substantial. If you leave the country before the expiry of the licence, you can obtain a refund by completing a form on the website.

Note that if you are only using your television set to watch subscription services like Netflix or Amazon Prime, a TV license is not required. It is only required if you watch or record live TV on any device or channel, including BBC iPlayer. 'Any device' includes laptops, tablets and mobiles.

Digital and satellite

One of the benefits of having digital television is that, in addition to the five terrestrial channels available with your television licence (i.e. BBC 1, BBC 2, ITV, Channel 4 and Channel 5), a digital Freeview box (freeview.co.uk) will allow you access to a host of free digital channels (*see Freeview section in this chapter*).

Additional cable, digital and satellite television may be available in your area through a service provider. Digital providers include BT, Virgin Media, Sky Digital and NowTV. Digital offers several advantages to the viewer such as widescreen pictures, CD-quality sound and video-on-demand.

Interactive services such as home banking, home shopping and connection to the Internet are also now available digitally through the television in some areas. Packages of televisions and DVD accessories are available to rent from Boxclever (boxclever.co.uk). In order to receive satellite communications, you may either purchase or rent an individual satellite dish to be installed at your residence. You must then subscribe to a plan, which will be payable on a monthly basis. Satellite dishes are available from many local high street electronic and appliance shops as well as from signal suppliers. To subscribe to channels such as CNN, MTV and Sky, contact Sky, Virgin Media, TalkTalk or BT.

DID YOU KNOW?

Some residential estates offer satellite TV reception via a central dish. Other buildings do not allow satellite dishes at all. Be sure to check before purchasing this service.

Freeview

A less expensive alternative to pay for digital television services or satellite television is called Freeview. This digital TV service requires that you purchase an electronic Freeview box (usually starting from £20), which you hook up to your television and aerial. There is no contract and no additional fees other than the cost of the Freeview box. Freeview boxes are available at your local electrical retailer.

Freeview digital television provides access to nearly 50 television channels, including all-day children's programming and round-the-clock news as well as several digital radio stations. Other options are Freeview+, which allows you to record digital television, and Freeview HD for high definition digital 5 television viewing. Some newer digital televisions include Freeview and a separate box does not need to be purchased. For more information: freeview.co.uk.

ELECTRICITY & GAS

Electricity and gas meters are generally read quarterly and bills are sent following the reading. The bill will include electricity units used and their unit price plus a quarterly standing charge. Electricity and gas services are not disconnected between renters. Make sure to take a gas and electricity meter reading during the move-in inspection to avoid being liable for charges incurred prior to move-in. Many gas and electric companies offer a dual fuel plan, usually less expensive than separate gas and electricity plans.

Gas is the least expensive method of heating. If you intend to install gas appliances, you should choose a registered gas fitter.

Gas water heaters

If you have individual gas water heaters (generally referred to as gas boilers in the UK) for bathrooms or the kitchen, you must have them serviced every year and make sure the rooms are well ventilated. A significant number of fatal accidents have occurred because of defective gas heaters.

Electricity supply

The electrical supply in the UK is 240V AC. Each electrical outlet has a switch to turn electricity on and off at the individual outlet. Keeping the switch off when not using that plug is a helpful tip to save on your electricity bill. The most common UK electrical plug is a square shaped, three-rectangular pin plug. This plug requires a fuse and has a ground wire (commonly referred to as an earth wire and appliances are earthed). The fuse is located inside the plug itself rather than at a central box.

Light bulbs

The UK has several types of light bulbs, including a screw-in and a pin variety. When purchasing replacement bulbs, you will need to know the type of bulb the lamp requires. It is often useful to bring the old bulb with you to the store as there are a great variety of bulbs.

WATER

Thames Water supplies water for most of London (thameswater.co.uk). Many water bills are not based on a consumption rate but on the value of the property plus a standing charge. Usually, you can improve on your water bill if your home is fitted with a water meter, which Thames Water will fit free of charge. You may not use a sprinkler to water your garden unless you have a water meter.

Water bills are sent semi-annually and include charges for water plus sewage services. You can call Thames Water to change your bills to quarterly or monthly cycles. If you rent your property, the landlord may pay this charge. In some houses, the only drinkable tap water is from the tap in the kitchen. Water from other taps may come from storage tanks on the premises, rather than from the main line.

You may find that the water in London is hard so you can use a decalcification liquid to rid appliances such as kettles, irons and washers of the limescale that accumulates with use. For your washing machine, water-softening tablets are available. For your dishwasher, salt is used to soften and prevent the deposit and stain of limescale on kitchen utensils. For both washing machines and dishwashers you can purchase anti-limescale tablets to use in your machines monthly.

If your water looks cloudy, discoloured, tastes different or smells funny, contact the Drinking Water Inspectorate: dwi.gov.uk.

RECYCLING & WASTE

Recycling centres for bottles, cans, clothes and paper products are widespread in London. Several methods of recycling are available to most London residents. These include doorstep recycling collection, blue bins (larger recycling bins found throughout London neighbourhoods in designated areas), mini recycling centres and composting.

Most residents receive one or two domestic waste collections each week and one weekly recycling collection. Normal refuse should be put in strong plastic bags and securely tied. There are usually no domestic collections on bank holidays, but be sure to check with your local council for further information. Most local councils also operate a *Too Big for the Bin* service for items that are too bulky to fit in with your normal refuse. Payment must be made in advance and can usually be made by credit and debit card, cash, cheques or postal orders. This service tends to be fairly popular and you may face a significant wait. Many councils also operate local tips (dumps) where you can take waste directly via car with specific points to dispose of, or recycle, garden waste, large appliances, computers and textiles. For specific details on all of the recycling and waste services available in your area, contact your local council (see *Local councils section* in this chapter). Also note that much of London has an urban fox problem (foxes are London's answer to North America's racoons) so it is best if rubbish is stored in bins or double bagged in order to prevent your rubbish becoming a midnight feast!

POST OFFICE & ROYAL MAIL

Royal Mail Holdings is a public corporation owned in part, but not managed, by the UK Government. Royal Mail Holdings includes three separate businesses: Post Office, Royal Mail and Parcelforce Worldwide. Post Office manages the post office outlets, Royal Mail is the branch that handles the delivery of all mail within the UK and Parcelforce Worldwide handles the movement of mail to and from overseas destinations.

Post Office

The Post Office has a very helpful website at royalmail.com. Here you can locate your local Post Office branch, track and trace mail posted in the UK, locate a UK address and learn about all of the services provided at your local Post Office. The Post Office has a nationwide network of about 12,000 offices. Most are open Monday to Friday from 09:00 to 17:30 and on Saturday from 09:00 to 12:30, although increasingly in central London Post Office branches are extending their hours. Neighbourhood Post Office hours vary with some open later on Saturdays.

The UK postal service provides a wider range of functions than in most other countries, offering over 170 products and services that include the following (note that services may vary from branch to branch):

- Banking. Basic banking services are available to customers at most high street branches of the Post Office.

- Certifying documents. Photocopies of identity documents certified as being a true likeness of the original.

- Credit cards, mortgages and personal loans, from £2,000 to £25,000.

- Driving licences and car tax application forms.

- Home phone and broadband plans.

- Insurance. Car, home, travel and pet insurance among others.

- Pay household bills. All payments such as phone, digital TV, utilities and council tax can be processed.

- Pay Self Assessment. Make your Self Assessment (tax return) payment by cheque, cash or debit card without charge. Be sure to take the Self Assessment payslip with you or else you will be charged for this service.

- Postal orders. Available at all branches of the Post Office. These can be used to pay household bills, pay someone who does not have access to a current (cheque) account and to send money domestically or internationally.

- Transferring money overseas. MoneyGram is a fast and safe way to send and receive money around the world in minutes. However, this service can be quite expensive and is best suited for urgent small transfers.

- Travel services. Foreign currency exchange and/or pre-order currency service, American Express travellers cheques, travel insurance and passport validation service.

Other Post Office services

Mail redirection service

The Post Office enables you to have mail redirected for a duration of three, six, or twelve months for a variable fee. This service is renewable for up to two years. Mail can be redirected to a permanent or temporary address, either within the UK or abroad. Fill out a redirection form at the post office (or download it from the website) at least a couple of weeks in advance of your move.

Keepsafe

The Post Office can hold your household's mail safely while you are away for up to two months and then deliver it on a day that you specify. The Post Office requires at least one week's notice for this service and charges a fee.

PO Box

As an alternative to receiving mail at home, you can set up a PO Box. You will be required to have a permanent UK home or work address. You can apply for a PO Box and find out about the full terms and conditions of the service by contacting your local Sales Centre.

Poste restante (holding mail)

Mail can be received free of charge via the main Post Office of any town in the UK. The mail will be returned to the sender if you do not collect it within 14 days (one month if sent from abroad). Photo identification is necessary when you collect the mail. This service can be quite useful if you are going to be living at a certain address for a short amount of time.

Royal Mail

Royal Mail collects, sorts and delivers the mail. Royal Mail provides a wide range of services, including signature on delivery, guaranteed next working day delivery and extra compensation cover for loss, damage or delay.

Sending mail

Postage stamps can be bought at the Post Office, grocery stores, newsagents and even some petrol stations. A pre-paid envelope can be recognised by the two thick vertical bars it has on the top right-hand side.

Sending mail within the UK

Two rates apply for sending letters in the UK up to 100 grams. First Class post will usually arrive the next business day within the UK. Second Class post is used for sending less-urgent items and usually takes about three business days for delivery. Recorded Signed For post provides additional reassurance by allowing for confirmation of delivery of important (but not valuable) items. You will receive proof of posting, signature on delivery, online confirmation of delivery and up to the value of 100 First Class stamps in compensation. You can track the progress and check if an item has been delivered on royalmail.com.

Special Delivery is available for the next day and by 09:00 the next working day. Special Delivery is recommended for valuable and time-sensitive items. This service provides the following benefits:

- up-to-date delivery tracking.
- a record of time and signature upon delivery (not necessarily the addressee's).
- confirmation of delivery by visiting royalmail.com.
- compensation up to £500 with the option to buy additional cover.

Sending mail abroad

Airmail items need a blue airmail sticker (supplied for free by the Post Office) or BY AIRMAIL – PAR AVION written in the top left-hand corner on the front of the item. The maximum weight for overseas postcards or letters is 2kg and all post goes by air.

A convenient and economical way to send goods and gifts is via the small packet service. When using this service, write SMALL PACKET in the top left-hand corner on the front of the item. A customs declaration form must also be attached. The maximum weight you can send is 2kg or less depending on the destination.

A cost-effective way to send printed papers such as pamphlets, books, magazines and newspapers abroad is the printed papers service. When using this service, write PRINTED PAPERS in the top left corner on the front of the item. You can't include personal correspondence. The maximum weight for most places is 2kg or 5kg for books and pamphlets.

International signed

This service allows you to send insured packages and ensure a signature is recorded upon delivery. This service is not available for all countries and the maximum compensation may be lower for some countries. Visit royalmail.com for more details.

Airsure is Royal Mail's fastest international tracked service. Mail is placed on the next available flight to the required destination. Airsure does not guarantee delivery times as postal standards vary from country to country. A variety of parcel services are offered depending on how fast you want the package to be delivered. A customs declaration form must be attached to the parcel. Parcelforce Worldwide provides a worldwide delivery service to over 200

countries. More information can be found at
parcelforce.com.

> *DID YOU KNOW?*
>
> *Postal services experience a surge in the volume of mail they handle during the holiday period so be sure to double check the final posting date for any Christmas/holiday packages and cards to ensure they will arrive in time.*

SENDING GOODS INTO THE UK

Care should be taken regarding the shipment of goods into the UK. Customs services may stop incoming shipments and levy VAT charges and import duties on the value of the incoming shipment. Should this happen, you will be required to pay the duty and a service charge before your package will be released for collection.

Chapter 6:

Transportation

There are a myriad of options for getting around London. Travelling around London is probably easiest and most enjoyable when wandering the streets and taking in the sights, smells and sounds. Like most major cities, London is often congested with traffic and travel by car, bus and taxi can be slow at peak times. For most journeys, the public transportation system is quite comprehensive and is made easier to manage by Oyster cards and Travelcards (London's electronic ticketing systems). The underground rail system (Tube), trains and buses can take you almost anywhere you want to go. The most useful resource for planning a trip by public transportation is the Transport for London (TfL) website (tfl.gov.uk). Transport for London (TfL) is the transport authority responsible for meeting the strategy and commitments regarding transport in London.

WALKING

The best way to get to know London is on foot. Most people now rely on a maps app on their smartphone to navigate the city – there are many to choose from and every Londoner has their favourite. Should you prefer a physical map, the *London A to Z Street Atlas* is the classic choice.

DID YOU KNOW?

Unlike the United States, where a zip code can cover a whole neighbourhood or town, postcodes in the UK correspond to a limited number of addresses or a single delivery point. Postcodes can also give an indication as to what part of the city an address is located and how far away from the centre of London it is (e.g., EC and WC are the closest to central London).

Remember that cars travel on the left side of the road, so pay attention when crossing to the writing on the street telling you to 'look right' or 'look left' as traffic may not be coming from the direction you expect. Also, when the traffic light is green, pedestrians do not have the right of way unless the pedestrian crossing light is green. Zebra crossing (a pedestrian crosswalk), which is clearly marked with black and white stripes painted on the road surface or on poles and a flashing yellow light, is also a safe way to cross the street although you should still check both ways and make sure cars see you and are stopping before you start to cross.

Should you wish for a more insightful walking experience, there are many good sources of guided walks be they tours, books or apps and podcasts. A good reference is *City Walks: London: 50 Adventures on Foot* by Craig Taylor, which provides 50 cards detailing places of interest and attractions by neighbourhood.

CYCLING

Cycling is a great way to explore London's many parks and neighbourhoods, visit the weekly farmers' markets and even commute to work. In the past few years there have been great improvements made to London's cycle network thanks to the efforts put forth by the former Mayor of London to create fast, safe and convenient cycle routes and superhighways throughout the city.

The Cycle Hire scheme (otherwise affectionately known as 'Boris bikes'), launched in summer 2010, is a public bicycle-sharing scheme for short journeys in and around central London. You can hire a bicycle, pick it up from one of many docking stations throughout the city, use it as you like, then drop it off at the nearest docking station ready for the next person. There is a nominal fee to access the bicycles and rides up to 30 minutes are free (there are extra ride charges for bicycle hires longer than 30 minutes, depending on how long you keep the bicycle). For additional details and to sign up for a cycle hire membership and information about cycling in the city, visit: tfl.gov.uk (search *cycling*).

Sustrans, a sustainable transport charity, also offers a comprehensive online guide to cycling in London as well as the greater London area (sustrans.org.uk).

Many employers are also signed up for Cyclescheme, through which employees can get a bicycle tax-free. Employers purchase the bicycle at full retail price and employees "hire" the bicycle from their employers with an option to purchase it at market value at the end of the scheme. For more information, visit: cyclescheme.co.uk.

OYSTER CARDS AND TRAVELCARDS

Public transportation tickets can be purchased as either a single-use ticket or by using an Oyster card, London's travel smartcard. Generally, travel on tubes and buses within London will cost you less if you use an Oyster card. Oyster cards are valid on the Tube, buses, Docklands Light Railway (DLR), London Overground, trams, riverboats and certain National Rail services. It can be topped up (added to) when your season ticket expires or your pay-as-you-go balance runs low. If you are making multiple journeys in a single day, the Oyster card will cap the price you pay and it will be slightly cheaper than a one-day Travelcard or Bus & Tram Pass. Oyster cards can be ordered online from TfL or purchased at Underground and National Rail ticket windows and machines or newsagents displaying a red 'Pass Agent' sign. Make sure you register your Oyster card online to protect it in case your card is lost or stolen and to check your balance.

For further information regarding rules and regulations for using an Oyster Card, including free and discounted travel for eligible persons, please visit: tfl.gov.uk/oyster.

Various types of paper tickets and passes can be purchased, ranging from single-ride tickets to Travelcards However, in almost all cases you are benefited financially by using an Oyster travelcard or pay-as-you-go.

For visitors to London, visitor Oyster cards are available. For further information, consult the TfL website or speak with a TfL representative at a local station.

DID YOU KNOW?

With the advent of contactless payment cards, it is now possible to pay-as-you-go on TfL using your debit or credit card. There is automatic fare capping for both daily and weekly travel.

Full details of all payment methods for TfL travel in London can be found at: tfl.gov.uk/fares.

UNDERGROUND

DID YOU KNOW?

London Underground, better known as the Tube, has 11 lines covering 402 kilometres and serving 270 stations. Opened in 1863, it is the world's oldest underground railway network and one of the largest.

Tube facts:

- Free paper maps are available at all London Transport ticket offices and the majority of the routes are clearly colour coded.

- Fares are based on the distance travelled.

- London is divided into six concentric bands called travel zones for Tube fares. Zones 1 and 2 are considered central London, while Zone 6 is the outer edges of London. The more zones you cross, the higher the fare.

- The Tube operates from approximately 05:00 until 12am-1am, Monday to Saturday, with reduced timetables on Sunday and public holidays.

- Rush hours (for peak fares) run from 06:30 to 09:30 and 16:00 – 19:00 Monday to Friday (excluding public holidays).

- Five Tube lines run a 24-hour service on Fridays and Saturdays – Victoria, Central, Jubilee, Northern and Piccadilly lines.

- Smoking and drinking alcohol are not permitted on the Underground trains or in the stations.

- Dogs are allowed to travel on the Underground and bicycles are allowed on most lines, although non-folding bikes are not allowed during peak hours.

- Stations and/or parts of the Tube lines may be closed due to construction/engineering works, especially at weekends, so it is always wise to check online before you begin your journey.

- If you forget to check for closures before you depart, look for the whiteboards at the station's entrance listing current service disruptions. You can also ask any station workers (at the ticket window or in the station wearing an orange vest) or press the green button on the round information box if more information is needed.

DID YOU KNOW?

TfL has introduced 'Please offer me a seat' badges for users who are less able to stand but for whom the need might not be apparent. Similarly, 'Baby on Board' badges are available for pregnant women. In each case, these badges alert other riders to offer their seat when conditions are crowded. Further information and order forms are available via: tfl.gov.uk.

OVERGROUND

London's Overground rail network consists of four routes travelling through 21 of London's 33 boroughs. As with the Tube, fares are based on the distance travelled. It operates similar hours to the tube network and operates 24 hours on Fridays and Saturdays between New Cross Gate and Highbury & Islington (not including Whitechapel).

DOCKLANDS LIGHT RAILWAY (DLR)

The DLR is an automated light rail system predominantly servicing the Docklands area of London. The DLR extends north to Stratford, south to Lewisham, west to Bank and Tower Gateway and east to City Airport and Woolwich Arsenal. Fares for the DLR are the same as for the Tube and Overground. Oyster card holders must tap in and out for each journey. DLR-only stations do not have ticket barriers so you must tap in and out. Correct ticketing is enforced by on-board checks. The DLR operates from approximately 05:30 to 00:30 Monday to Saturday with reduced timetables on Sundays and public holidays. The DLR runs every 2 to 5 minutes on weekdays and 5 to 10 minutes on weekends.

BUSES

Buses are less expensive than the Underground. Most buses run from approximately 06:00 to midnight with different timetables on Sunday and public holidays. Several night bus routes operate after midnight until 06:00 to cover the period between when the Tube closes and the start of the daytime bus services. Trafalgar Square is the hub for most night bus routes.

Most bus stops have signs indicating which bus routes stop there. Some stops are 'request stops', which are marked with red signs. It is always best practice to signal the driver from the road that you wish to board the bus by holding out your hand. Cash cannot be used to purchase a bus fare, you must have a day travelcard, an Oyster or contactless payment card or a bus and tram travelcard. If using an Oyster or contactless payment card, your fare will never exceed the daily or weekly maximum. Full details can be found on the TfL website (tfl.gov.uk) bus information page.

COACHES

Victoria Coach Station, London's main coach station, is located at 164 Buckingham Palace Road, SW1W. The station supports all forms of coach activities, including scheduled express and commuter services, coach holidays and private hire. It is the base for many coach operators and is equipped with services including a travel counter and luggage storage facilities.

The following are a few of the major coach operators. These companies link London with other cities in the United Kingdom, Ireland and Continental Europe.

- National Express Coaches: nationalexpress.com

- Megabus: uk.megabus.com

- Green Line: greenline.co.uk

TRAINS

Modern, high-speed trains (mainline service) link the major cities in the UK. There are also commuter lines (local service) between towns and outlying areas. Tickets can be purchased at any train station, online or by phone and at most travel agencies. If you have an Oyster card or Travelcard, it may be valid for train journeys that are within Zones 1-9. Otherwise, there are various ticket schemes. Anytime fares are flexible tickets with no time restrictions on when you can travel, off-peak fares are cheaper tickets for travelling on trains during off-peak hours on specified dates and advance fares are single (one-way) tickets that offer great value but require reservations and are subject to availability.

Several discount Railcards (e.g. 16-25, Family & Friends, Network, Senior, Disabled and HM Forces) are sold for an annual fee where holders get one-third off all standard class tickets, subject to certain restrictions. You should ask about the most economical way to get to your destination before purchasing a ticket.

If your journey involves both National Rail and Tube or DLR services, you can pay a through fare that is valid for the entire trip. When you buy your ticket, you will need to supply your final destination and state that you plan to travel using a combination of services. Hold on to your ticket throughout the duration of your journey.

For more information, visit: nationalrail.co.uk.

Tickets may also be purchased in advance from: thetrainline.com.

Trains for various destinations in the UK depart from the following London stations:

- North & Central Britain, Scotland & Continental

  o Europe Euston, King's Cross, St. Pancras International

- The South & Southeast

  o Charing Cross, London Bridge, Victoria, Waterloo

- The West Country, Wales & South Midlands

  o Paddington, Waterloo, Marylebone

- The East, East Anglia & Essex

  o Liverpool Street, Victoria, Fenchurch Street

Express trains to London airports

The fastest way to get to most of London's airports is via the express trains listed next.

- Heathrow Express/Heathrow Connect
  - Paddington
- Gatwick Express
  - Victoria
- Stansted Express
  - Liverpool Street or Tottenham Hale

Note: It is also quite easy and inexpensive to take the underground directly to Heathrow on the Piccadilly Line.

RIVER BUS

London's river services provide reliable (and enjoyable!) transportation for both commuter and leisure journeys along the Thames River. Commuter services are available from Woolwich Arsenal Pier in the east to Embankment Pier in the west as well as Blackfriars Pier in the City to Putney Pier in the west.

KPMG Thames Clippers (thamesclippers.com) has a fleet of hi-speed catamarans that leave the major piers every 20 minutes starting at approximately 06:00 and ending around 01:00 the following day.

Thames Clippers also offers the O2 Express, a limited stop service from Waterloo London Eye Pier to the North Greenwich Pier. Very useful if travelling to or from the O2 for an event or concert!

BLACK CABS

The familiar black London taxi (now often painted in other colours yet still commonly referred to as the black cab) is the most expensive but often the most convenient and reliable form of transportation. All licensed London taxi drivers need to pass a special test (the Knowledge), which usually takes between two and four years, before they can drive a black cab.

Taxis are strictly controlled by law and all areas within London are regulated by meters. The meter calculates the maximum fare based on time of day, distance travelled and taxi speed. Many taxis can now accept credit or debit cards. However there may be a surcharge of 10 to 15 percent on the metered fare. During periods of fare increases and before meters are adjusted, your fare may be higher than the meter indicates but the new fares will be explained and posted inside the cab. It is customary to tip by rounding up the charge (e.g., pay £6 for a £5.50 fare) or by giving approximately 10 percent. Taxis are limited by law to carrying five adults. If you are travelling with children, it is worth knowing that infants and small children can ride in black cabs sitting in a buggy/stroller using the wheelchair space. You can hail a taxi that has a lit 'for hire' sign on its roof, queue (line up) at an appointed taxi stand or ring one of the taxi companies directly.

MINICABS

London also has minicabs, taxis that can be both licensed and unlicensed. Minicabs cannot be hailed in the street and must be booked ahead of time. Any minicab journey that isn't booked by phone or in a minicab office is illegal and risky. If a minicab stops you in the street and offers you a ride, you should always refuse the offer.

Booking your minicab guarantees that your trip will be carried out by a licensed driver in a licensed vehicle. It is important to verify or even negotiate a minicab price when you book and it is helpful to have a good idea of where you are going as minicab drivers (unlike black cab drivers) are not required to know London streets and directions. Most minicab drivers will have SatNav (GPS) to assist them.

One of the most popular, reputable and trustworthy minicab services is Addison Lee, which can be booked by phone or online (addisonlee.com). Additionally, on-demand app-based taxi services are available in London, Uber being the most popular.

DRIVING IN THE UK

Owning a car is not essential in central London because of the comprehensive public transportation. If you prefer the convenience of a car, you can buy, lease or rent a vehicle easily. It is strongly recommended that you purchase and read *The*

Highway Code, the official road user guide for Great Britain (available in most bookshops or online, which outlines the British driving regulations before beginning to drive in Britain. The differences do not end with driving on the left-hand side of the road!).

Congestion charge

As in any other major city, traffic and congestion are problems in London. In an effort to reduce congestion and encourage the use of other modes of transport in London, certain vehicles must pay a congestion charge when driving within central London between 07:00 and 18:00, Monday to Friday. The Congestion Charging Zone is clearly marked with traffic signs, including a large letter 'C' in a red circle, and there are cameras monitoring every entrance and exit.

The Congestion Charge does not apply on weekends, bank holidays, or the three working days between Christmas and New Year. Residents who live within the Congestion Charging Zone receive a discount on the Congestion Charge. Certain vehicles (e.g., alternative fuel and electrically propelled vehicles) are exempt from the Congestion Charge.

The Congestion Charge can be paid online, by text message or phone, by post or at newsagents, petrol stations and any other shop displaying the 'C' sign. For more detailed and up-to-date information regarding the congestion charge, exemptions and to pay online, visit: tfl.gov.uk (search *Congestion Charge*).

Driving licences

It is important to obtain a proper driving licence, because driving without one is illegal and will affect your insurance. For people moving from the US, you are able to drive for up to 12 months on your US license. For more information regarding licences and current regulations related to transferring your licence from abroad, visit the website of the Driver and Vehicle Licensing Agency (DVLA), part of the Department of Transport: dvla.gov.uk.

Insurance

In the UK, the driver needs to be insured to use a specified vehicle rather than the vehicle being insured for use by specified persons. Third party insurance is compulsory and it is advisable to have comprehensive insurance as well. 'No claims' reductions and other options are available. You might bring a letter from your previous insurance agency stating that you are entitled to no claims insurance for the past five years. It is recommended that you contact several insurance companies regarding types of coverage and cost. You should also have a clear understanding with your insurance company regarding claims and the kind of licence you possess.

Purchasing a car

Purchasing a car in Britain is expensive but there is a good market for second-hand cars. An online search can yield a number of official second-hand car sellers. Autotrader (autotrader.co.uk) and Car Giant (cargiant.co.uk) can be good starting points. Both the Automobile Association (AA) and the Royal Automobile Club (RAC) will thoroughly inspect and value second-hand cars for their members for a fee. See automobile associations in this chapter.

A compulsory Road Tax must be paid each year for each car. This can be done online at: gov.uk/vehicle-tax.

If your car is more than three years old, you must have a Ministry of Transport (MOT) test each year to prove its roadworthiness. Garages licensed by the MOT to conduct this test can perform the test within 24 hours or while you wait. There is a fee for this service. You must present your MOT certificate along with proof of insurance when paying your Road Tax.

Leasing, renting and sharing cars

Leasing cars is a common practice in the UK and dealers can supply details of the various lengths of time and conditions. Car hire firms provide the usual services. Cars with manual transmission are most common and less expensive than those with automatic transmissions. Car rental companies are listed in the Yellow Pages of the phone directory under

Car Rental or Car Hire – Self Drive. Hertz, Avis, Budget, Enterprise, Europcar, Kenning and Thrifty are well-known rental agencies.

Car Clubs are another option that enables you to hire a car by the hour (or longer stretches) with pickups available all over most London neighbourhoods. These self-service car hire companies require you to become a member by paying an annual fee. You can then reserve a car online, via phone or smartphone app and for pick up at one of the many convenient locations all over London. In addition to use of the car, rates generally cover petrol, insurance and congestion charge. Available cars vary in size from a Smart car to family size. For further information, visit: tfl.gov.uk/modes/driving/car-clubs.

Automobile associations

You may consider becoming a member of the Automobile Association (AA) or the Royal Automobile Club (RAC). These organisations offer emergency services, breakdown insurance for trips to the Continent and can even provide legal service in court.

- The Automobile Association: theaa.com
- The Royal Automobile Club Motoring Services: rac.co.uk

Parking

Parking is limited to car parks (parking lots) or meters for non-residents in certain areas and street parking in these restricted areas is only possible for residents with permits (resident's parking). In many areas of London, you are entitled to purchase a Resident's Parking Permit (check with your council for eligibility). Traffic wardens regularly patrol residential areas and fines are given if you are in a restricted area without the proper parking permit. Resident parking regulations vary from area to area so it is imperative to read signs thoroughly.

If you are not fortunate enough to locate a parking meter on the street, you may opt for a car park. Blue signs with a white 'P' direct you to public parking in unfamiliar surroundings. Central public parking garages can be found through the NCP (National Car Parks) website: ncp.co.uk.

Clamping

Parking violations may result in fines, towing or clamping (where a triangular metal trap is fitted over one car wheel preventing the car from moving), all of which involve considerable expense and inconvenience. In the unfortunate case of getting clamped, you can call your local council to have it removed. Vehicles may also be clamped or removed as a result of TfL's congestion charging scheme. Drivers unsure of whether a vehicle has been clamped and towed should consult the TRACE website: trace.london.

HELPFUL APPS

London can be daunting, particularly when you are getting to know the city. Luckily, there are a number of useful smartphone applications to cover all of your transportation needs while you are out and about.

- London A to Z

  o Digital edition of the A to Z available for download to iPhone, iPad, Android and Windows Phone 7. A good alternative to Google Maps.

- Google Maps

  o Available for iPhone, iPad and Android.

- Citymapper

  o Shows walking, public transport, bicycle and taxi options including fare, calories burned and travel time. Available for iPhone and Android.

- Busmapper

  o Shows nearest bus stops and routing options. Available for iPhone and Android.

- London Tube Map

  o Map of the London Underground and live travel status. Available for iPhone, iPad and Android.

- Santander Cycles

  o Official app for the Santander Cycle Hire scheme shows nearest docking stations and availability. Available for iPhone, iPad and Android.

- Hailo

  o Uses GPS to hail a black cab to your current location. Also allows you to automatically pay by credit or debit card. Available for iPhone and Android.

- Addison Lee

  o Make minicab bookings via smartphone for as soon as possible or a specified time. Available for iPhone, Blackberry, Nokia, Windows Phone 7 and Android.

- Kabbee

  o Minicab bookings throughout London. Available for iPhone and Android.

- National Rail Enquiries

  o Provides live train information, timetables and station information. Available for iPhone, iPad and Android.

- Heathrow Express

  o Purchase and receive tickets on your smartphone. Also provides timetables and live service updates. Available for iPhone, Blackberry and Android

- Uber

  o Hail Uber rides, see if there are drivers local to you, and an approximate cost of an average ride to your chosen destination.

Pin It! Best places to try Fish & Chips

Now that you have an idea of how to get there, we recommend trying a London staple – Fish and Chips. Three of our Junior League of London favourites are:

- <u>Golden Union Fish Bar</u>, 38 Poland Street (Soho)

- <u>The Fish House of Notting Hill</u>, 29 Pembridge Road, (Notting Hill)

- <u>The Sea Shell of Lisson Grove</u>, 49 Lisson Grove (Marylebone)

Chapter 7:

Healthcare

Public healthcare in the UK is provided by the National Health Service (NHS). It provides excellent care and is low-cost or free of charge for UK citizens and most foreign-born UK residents. Private healthcare is also available across the UK. Access to private healthcare is acquired by means of private health insurance (often available through employers) or paid directly by customers. Some doctors see patients both privately and under the NHS.

This chapter explains the services provided by NHS and private healthcare centres and lists contact details and information for both. It is essential to have healthcare in the UK, so if you do not qualify for healthcare under the NHS, you should ensure that you are covered privately. Many Londoners, even if they do qualify for NHS healthcare, choose to be covered privately as well, as the NHS can have waiting lists for non-urgent operations and specialists.

Should you require a visit from a private doctor at a place and time that is convenient to you, 24 hours a day, seven days a week, contact Doctorcall: doctorcall.co.uk.

For full details of NHS care visit: nhs.uk

FOR AN AMBULANCE IN SERIOUS EMERGENCY

DIAL 999

ACCIDENT & EMERGENCY (A&E) UNITS

In the event of an emergency, go directly to the nearest hospital with an A&E unit. For minor injuries and illnesses, NHS walk-in centres and minor injuries clinics provide treatment seven days a week. You do not need an appointment and will be seen by an experienced NHS nurse. There are walk-in centres located throughout the city and in many residential areas. To locate the walk-in centre nearest to you, visit the NHS website (nhs.uk). Additionally, for non-urgent medical queries you can phone 111, a free NHS health line that can help determine the best course of action for your current ailment.

NATIONAL HEALTH SERVICE (NHS)

The NHS is government-subsidised. If you pay National Insurance (NI) as a resident of the UK, you are entitled to medical coverage at little or no additional cost. This service includes:

- doctor care, including home visits if necessary.
- specialist and hospital care.
- dentistry and orthodontic care.
- eye examinations and glasses.
- child-care clinics for under-fives.
- maternity care.
- well-man and well-woman clinics.
- marriage counselling.
- family planning services.

While most of the services are free of charge, there are some (e.g. prescriptions, sight tests and dental treatments) that incur a supplementary charge.

DID YOU KNOW?

In the UK, specialists and general practitioners are addressed as Doctor. Surgeons, including dental surgeons, obstetricians and gynaecologists, are referred to as Mr, Mrs, or Miss. The surgery or operating room in a hospital is called a theatre and the office of a medical professional is called a surgery.

NHS registration

All permanent UK residents are eligible to register with the NHS. Eligibility for temporary residents depends on whether you or your spouse is paying UK income tax and National Insurance (NI).

To obtain an NHS number, you must register with a doctor or General Practitioner (GP) who has vacancies for NHS patients. To be eligible for care with a particular GP surgery, you must live within the catchment area of the surgery. Note: not all GPs handle NHS patients, some handle only private patients. It is up to the discretion of the GP to register temporary residents with the NHS.

For a complete listing of GP surgeries in your area, visit: nhs.uk. The website will provide an address, phone number and map and may identify whether or not the GP is accepting new NHS patients. As an alternative, contact your local council for the names, addresses and telephone numbers of GPs in your area.

There are often waiting lists for NHS doctors. In those cases, it may be easiest to sign up with a local GP practice as a private patient and ask to be placed on their NHS waiting list. This may be the best way to get into the local practice of your choice.

For medical attention other than general family care, you must be referred by your GP. Known in the UK as a consultant, the specialist is anyone other than a GP. Most consultants practise under the NHS and privately. Due to the nature of public health care, it is possible that in non-emergency cases you will be required to go on a waiting list before being seen by a health professional (this includes non-emergency operations). In these instances, consulting a private doctor may be preferable as there would be no waiting list. Under certain circumstances, both NHS and private doctors are willing to make house calls.

PRIVATE MEDICAL CARE

An alternative to NHS medical care is private treatment. Although much more costly, it allows you to have control over when treatment should take place and who should perform it. Visit privatehealth.co.uk for more information.

Employer-sponsored group health plans issued in other countries may be extended to the UK with employer consent. Any questions regarding the extent of coverage should be directed to your employer's HR department. You may wish to consider subscribing to a British form of medical insurance. BUPA and AXA PPP are two of the most popular plans. These insurance plans generally cover hospital and specialist treatment but not routine visits to the GP or dentist as the NHS covers these.

There are around 50 privately-staffed and run hospitals in the London area. These facilities are available to private-care patients only. These hospitals offer private rooms and overall good facilities. However, they may not offer the same emergency care as NHS hospitals and are not subject to the same regulation. A few of the more well-known places are listed below.

- The Harley Street Clinic: theharleystreetclinic.com

  o Specialists in cancer and cardiology treatments.

- The Lister Hospital:.thelisterhospital.com

  o Known for its assisted conception and fertility clinic.

- The London Clinic: thelondonclinic.co.uk

  o Largest single private hospital in the UK.

- The Princess Grace Hospital: theprincessgracehospital.com

PRESCRIPTIONS

Doctors write prescriptions to be filled at a chemist (pharmacy). You will be required to pay a fixed cost for each prescription unless the patient for whom the prescription is written in is within a class of persons who receive prescriptions at no cost, including but not limited to, persons under 16 years old, full-time students under 19 years old and pensioners.

Oral contraception is free in most cases and you may ask your doctor if you are eligible. In addition, women holding a Maternity Exemption Certificate (obtained from your doctor during pregnancy) will receive free prescriptions during pregnancy and for one year after the birth of the baby.

People with regular prescriptions may find it cost-effective to buy a prepayment certificate (PPC). Speak with your doctor for further information or consult the NHS website (nhs.uk).

DENTAL CARE

Dental care is available through the NHS (much the same as medical care) at a reduced cost. As an NHS dental patient, you are expected to pay a percentage of the cost of any procedures required. There is an upper limit set on the contribution you will be asked to make for one course of treatment.

Expect to be asked to pay all or part of the charge in advance. Before each and every visit, you must ascertain that the dentist will treat you as an NHS patient otherwise you could be treated as a private patient. It is also worth noting that dental hygienists performing routine cleaning are not covered by the NHS.

If you are interested in trying to locate a dentist using the NHS, lists of NHS dentists are posted in the same fashion as NHS doctors via the NHS website (nhs.uk). Centrally-located private dental clinics:

- Carnaby Street Dental Practice: carnabystreetdentist.co.uk

- Weymouth Street Paediatric Dentistry: paediatric-dentistry.co.uk

EYE CARE

Your eyes can be tested by a registered ophthalmic optician (optometrist) or an ophthalmic medical practitioner. Free sight tests are available to some, consult the NHS website (nhs.uk) for full details.

The optician must give you a prescription (or a certificate that you do not need glasses), even if your sight has not changed. You cannot be asked to pay for your sight test until you have been given your prescription. You are under no obligation to buy your eyeglasses from the same optician who gave you the test. Your prescription is valid for two years. If you need to consult with an ophthalmologist (a medical doctor with knowledge on diseases of the eye), visit: moorfields.nhs.uk.

MATERNITY CARE

If you are expecting a baby in the UK, you will need to decide whether to have your baby on the NHS or privately. It is important to note that most UK private health insurers do not consider pregnancy a medical condition and do not cover antenatal (prenatal), delivery and postnatal care unless you have a high-risk condition. However, some private health insurance policies specialise in maternity coverage for expats living in the UK.

NHS

With the NHS, all maternity care is free of charge. The first step is to tell your GP or local midwifery clinic. A booking appointment will then be made for you. This should take place by the time you are 10 weeks pregnant. With straightforward pregnancies, antenatal care usually consists of a series of appointments with a community midwife and occasionally, your GP. Appointments usually take place at your local clinic, operated by a team of midwives. You will probably see more than one midwife during your antenatal visits. Your antenatal care may also be shared between the community midwives and your GP (shared care). The midwife may visit you at home for antenatal checks and you may go into hospital for any special tests.

You will also be offered a dating scan (around 12 weeks) that will also include the nuchal translucency scan combined with blood tests and an anomaly scan (around 20 weeks) to ensure that your baby is developing properly. Provided there are no issues, no other scans are required.

When it comes to your baby's birth, you can choose to give birth in hospital, at a midwife-led birth centre or at home (an increasingly popular option in the UK). In the UK, babies are usually delivered by midwives. However, maternity units are fully supported by doctors in case of complications. There are no guarantees that you will have met the midwives who help to deliver your baby but all of your important information will be in your notes. If complications do arise, you will be transferred to consultant care.

In hospital, you will have a private birthing room but will be transferred to an NHS ward for recovery (which usually have four to eight beds). Private or semi-private rooms are sometimes available for recovery and usually cost around £500 per night. With straightforward deliveries, you will usually be free to go home from around six hours after delivery (once breastfeeding has been established and the baby has been checked).

After you have had your baby, whether using the NHS or private healthcare, a midwife will come to your home after you have given birth to check that you and your baby are healthy and adjusting to life at home. The midwife will schedule visits with you for up to ten days after the birth (or longer if deemed necessary).

Following a new mum's discharge from the midwife's services, a health visitor (a specially-trained nurse concerned with the health of the whole family) will visit the home to offer help and support. You may continue to see the health visitor periodically for general questions on the baby's growth, feeding and other common baby questions. You will often see your health visitor at baby weigh in clinics where you can ask questions about development and have the baby weighed to ensure growth is following a normal pattern.

Private care

With private maternity care (and depending on your insurance), you can choose to have antenatal care on the NHS and pay for private delivery or have private maternity care throughout your pregnancy and delivery. An advantage of private maternity care is that you will know the midwife and obstetrician who will attend the birth of your baby.

For a normal delivery with no complications, delivery at a private maternity hospital in London under an obstetrician usually costs around £5,000 for one night (not including antenatal care or any complications). In the case of an unexpected emergency situation, there is always an obstetrician on call in both private and NHS hospitals and it may result in an emergency transfer to an NHS hospital (or ward if birthing in a hospital with both services). Private doctors may use both NHS and private hospital facilities. It is important to book early with a private obstetrician as they only take a limited number of patients per month and it is critical that you are comfortable with the style of the obstetrician. If you need to change obstetricians, it is better to do so earlier rather than later.

If your pregnancy is considered 'high risk', you may not be allowed to deliver your baby at a private hospital. Instead, you may have to deliver your baby at an NHS hospital that has more appropriate facilities to care for you and the baby in the case of an emergency. You may feel more comfortable knowing that at an NHS hospital there are more staff and facilities to handle unforeseen emergencies.

Independent midwives

Another option is to employ an independent midwife. This allows you the opportunity to get to know the midwife who will be present at the delivery of your baby. Private midwives usually offer monthly visits until 28 weeks, twice-weekly between 28 and 36 weeks and until the baby is born and a daily visit for the first 7-10 days after birth. Private midwives are able to attend home births or hospital births and provide assistance with establishing breastfeeding. Fees start at around £4,000 for antenatal care and delivery.

Hospitals with maternity wards

In London, most large hospitals offer good maternity facilities. Some hospitals with exceptional maternity facilities are listed below. Note that not all hospitals have neonatal intensive care units. If you choose private care, accommodation must be reserved well in advance of your baby's due date. Hospitals may also request a deposit at the time of reservation

- Chelsea & Westminster Hospital: chelwest.nhs.uk

  o Has excellent childbirth facilities including birthing pools and a private maternity wing (the Kensington Wing). NHS and private.

- Portland Hospital for Women and Children: theportlandhospital.com

  o Private

- Queen Charlotte's Maternity Hospital: imperial.nhs.uk

  o Has excellent childbirth facilities including birthing pools and a private maternity wing (the Sir Stanley Clayton Ward). NHS and private.

- St Mary's Hospital: imperial.nhs.uk

  o Has excellent childbirth facilities including birthing pools and a private maternity wing (the Lindo Wing – where Prince George was born!). NHS and private.

DID YOU KNOW?

Black cabs may refuse to transport you to hospital once in labour. If you are planning to deliver at a private hospital and need transportation, contact the hospital to arrange for a private transfer. If you call 999 or 112 for an ambulance, they must take you to the nearest hospital.

Antenatal classes

The NHS and most private hospitals offer parents birth and preparatory parenting classes at local hospitals and clinics. Most first-time mothers choose to take an antenatal course through the National Childbirth Trust (NCT). The NCT is a non-profit organisation formed expressly for the purpose of education for pregnancy, birth and parenthood. Contact the NCT for information on what parenting and birth preparation courses are offered in your area: nct.org.uk.

You must contact the NCT early in your pregnancy,

usually during the second trimester, if you are interested in antenatal classes in London. Many of the neighbourhood branches of the NCT have produced wonderful information packs on having a baby in London that can be a great help to a pregnant expatriate.

BIRTH REGISTRATION

All births taking place in the UK must be registered. The hospital where the birth occurs will notify the local Registrar of Births, Deaths and Marriages with details of the birth. The parents (mother or father, if the parents are legally married) must register the child at the local office within 42 days of the birth. Either a short- or long-form birth certificate is available for a fee. The long form is more detailed and, in some countries, it is considered to be the only 'official' birth certificate. Therefore, it is often helpful to obtain several official long-form birth certificates at the time of registration so that they are readily available when required (there is a discounted fee on the day of registration). It is recommended that babies born in the UK to resident foreign nationals register at the appropriate foreign embassy or high commission to receive proper citizenship papers and passports. Each country's laws differ, so it is best to check with your embassy's website. There is usually a fee for this service.

In certain circumstances, it will also be possible to register a child born in the UK as a UK national and obtain a British passport for the child. These include children born to parents who are legally settled in the UK at the time of the child's birth. However, this option may affect the child's primary citizenship. The Home Office website can furnish you with full details: gov.uk.

PAEDIATRIC CARE

Your local health clinic or GP offers a full service of paediatric care, as well as child health clinics that specialise in children only. Check with your local GP for one close to you. The following services are available:

- Vaccinations

- Developmental checks (e.g. hearing, vision, weight, height)

- Psychotherapy, educational psychology for learning and behaviour problems, speech therapy and orthopaedics.

- Health visitors who run clinics and/or make house calls to answer any questions you may have, discuss problems, remind you of injection dates and help direct you to local playgroups and registered childminders in your area.

All clinics have emergency numbers to be used after hours. GPs or their deputies will make house calls in emergency situations. A recommended private paediatric centre for round-the-clock, one-stop child healthcare is the Harley Street Paediatric Group: harleystreetpaediatricgroup.com.

VACCINATIONS

Vaccinations for children are available free of charge through your local GP or Child Health Clinic. The NHS vaccination schedule can be found on the NHS website (nhs.uk). Vaccinations that are not included in the NHS protocol are available for a fee, in some cases at your GP's office but more commonly at private providers including local pharmacies. Check with your local pharmacist or GP for further information.

FAMILY PLANNING

A full range of family planning services are available through your GP or local clinics as well as specific family planning clinics run by the NHS. The larger clinics will offer all types of birth control for men and women, well-women clinics, psycho-sexual counselling, termination referrals and follow-up and post-natal examinations. All services are available free of charge on a walk-in basis. To find your nearest clinic and further information contact The Family Planning Association: fpa.org.uk.

COUNSELLING

To find information about where to receive counselling locally, start by asking your GP. Some other useful addresses and telephone numbers:

- Alcoholics Anonymous: alcoholics-anonymous.org.uk

- British Association for Counselling and Psychotherapy (BACP): bacp.co.uk

- Counselling Directory: counselling-directory.org.uk

- Cruse Bereavement Care: cruse.org.uk

- Narcotics Anonymous: ukna.org

- Relate: relate.org.uk

- The Tavistock Centre for Couple Relationships: tavistockrelationships.org

- Family Lives: familylives.org.uk

COMPLEMENTARY MEDICINE

Your local health food store or chemist can be a good resource for complementary therapies and alternative health products (e.g., herbal supplements, vitamins and homeopathic products).

Below is a list of resources and centres where you may find a variety of complementary medicine products and practitioners, including acupuncture, homeopathy, osteopathy and reflexology.

- AcuMedic Centre: <u>acumedic.com</u>
- The Hale Clinic: <u>haleclinic.com</u>
- Holland & Barrett: <u>hollandandbarrett.com</u>
- Neal's Yard Remedies: <u>nealsyardremedies.com</u>
- The Royal London Hospital for Integrative Medicine:

<u>uclh.nhs.uk/OurServices/OurHospitals/RLHIM</u>.

Chapter 8:

Children

If life with children is an adventure, living in London with children is an even bigger one! Whether you already have children or are having a child here for the first time, the resources in this chapter will get you and your little ones started on exploring London and taking advantage of all it has to offer. There is no shortage of things to do in London for younger ones – it's just a matter of becoming familiar with all of the options and narrowing down the choices. Despite all of the various venues, activities and special events, you will not find one source that lists everything to do. You should also contact your local council and visit your local library, children's centres, parks, playgrounds and schools for more information. You will be amazed at what isn't advertised in the local newspaper or magazine!

BABY CARE PRODUCTS

Many popular foreign brands are widely available in the UK. However, you will find that the selection can vary depending on the store or chemist which means you may have to visit a few different places in order to find everything you're looking for.

Johnson & Johnson, Pampers and Huggies products are carried by most supermarket and chemist chains in the UK. Large supermarkets and chemists such as Sainsbury's, Tesco, Waitrose and Boots also carry their own lines of wipes and nappies. Anything you seek can also either be ordered through Amazon or, if you are particularly wedded to an American product, you can order to ship from Target's international site.

Vaseline and A+D ointment are sold in the UK. There are also several British-made nappy rash ointments, such as Sudocrem and Kamillosan, that work very well.

BREASTFEEDING/FORMULA FEEDING

Breastfeeding, while not the exclusive choice, is very popular in London. There are a number of resources available to support new mums. The most popular and widely distributed brands of feeding accessories are Avent, Dr Brown's and Tommee Tippee, offering everything from bottles and nipples to breast pumps, shields and storage bags. Medela breast pumps and accessories are readily available from Amazon and John Lewis.

Ready-to-feed or powdered infant formulas are commonly offered in the following brands: SMA, Cow & Gate, Aptamil, SMA Wysoy (a soya milk formula) and Hipp Organic. It is possible to find specialised formulas (such as hypoallergenic) but you may need to search a bit more as these items are generally not carried in most chemists or supermarkets. Specialised formulas are sometimes also available via prescription, so it is worth chatting with your GP if your child has a dietary restriction and needs specific formula.

It is worth noting that no formula is provided in hospital after birth unless medically required. If you do not intend to breastfeed, you must bring formula and feeding accessories with you to the hospital when you give birth. Additionally, you need to bring nappies (diapers) and wipes for your baby after birth as well as clothes, blankets, and dummies.

"MUMMY" SPEAK

Important terms to know for parents in the UK.

- antenatal = prenatal
- beaker = sippy cup
- cot = crib
- crèche = short-term childcare (e.g. at the gym or church)
- crib = cradle

- dummy = pacifier
- flannel = washcloth
- Moses basket = bassinet
- nappies = diapers
- plaster = band aid
- pram = buggy
- pushchair = stroller
- tea = children's supper/dinner
- teat = nipple (baby bottle)
- vest = t-shirt/undershirt

DID YOU KNOW?

UK bed and linen sizes (including those for baby cots) may vary from store to store as well as from any standard sizes in your home country.

BABY FOOD/FEEDING ITEMS

Popular UK brands of baby food include many organic brands such as Hipp Organic, Ella's and Organix. Beaker cups, bibs, feeding bowls and accessories are readily available at many supermarkets, chemists, department stores such as John Lewis and online.

DETERGENTS

Fairy, Ariel and Persil are common detergent brands found in stores and offer both biological and non-biological formulas. Many brands also offer a 'sensitive' formula. There is also a handy product called Napisan, which safely removes germs and stains from children's clothes. Napisan can be difficult to source in store and may need to be purchased online.

MEDICAL NEEDS

Baby first aid/safety

Below are some helpful contacts for baby first aid and safety information and training. The National Childbirth Trust (NCT nct.org.uk) also offers a variety of classes on baby care.

- The Babywebsite.com: thebabywebsite.com
- The Working Parent Company: theworkingparentcompany.co.uk

    o Offers classes in first aid and basic life support and can arrange private sessions in your home.

- The Portland Hospital: theportlandhospital.com

    o Offers a baby/toddler first aid class taught by a midwife. Topics include how to make your house safer, what to do in emergencies and how to administer CPR with practice on a manikin. Classes are held monthly.

- British Red Cross: redcross.org.uk,

  o Offers first aid classes at a variety of locations around the UK. Private classes can also be arranged for small groups.

Healthcare/immunisations

For more information on the NHS and paediatrics, see *Chapter 7: Healthcare*.

Medicines

Over-the-counter medicines for children's health are readily available, although they may carry different brand names than you are used to. Most chemist shops have a pharmacist on duty that can help you find the medicine you need for your situation.

Popular children's medicines and products include:

- Aqueous cream: dry skin
- Calpol: pain reliever containing paracetamol
- Canesten: antifungal cream
- Dentinox: teething pain
- Dioralyte: rehydration powder (to be mixed with water)
- E45 cream: dry skin

- Gripe water: colic and hiccups
- Infacol: colic
- Nurofen: pain reliever containing ibuprofen
- Oilatum: cradle cap, eczema
- Piriton syrup: antihistamine
- Sudocrem: nappy rash
- Zinc and castor oil lotion: nappy rash

Pregnancy

Pregnancy is discussed in more detail in *Chapter 7: Healthcare – Maternity care*

Maternity Clothing

The following stores sell a variety of maternity clothes. In addition, some major department stores and high street stores, such as Topshop, H&M and The Gap, offer a selection of maternity clothes – be sure to check locations to make sure there is a maternity department. In most cases, maternity wear is only stocked online. In addition, children's stores such as JoJo Maman Bébé, Mothercare and Mamas & Papas also sell maternity clothing (see *Shopping and services* in this chapter).

- Isabella Oliver: isabellaoliver.com
- Séraphine: seraphine.com

CHILDCARE

Childcare is readily available in London. There are, however, some distinctions from the United States in terminology and scope of care.

Au pair

A young person, usually a young woman in her late teens or early 20s and often from Europe, who lives with a family hoping to improve their command of English. She will help around the house and do some babysitting for up to 35 hours per week in exchange for her room and board and small salary. She is usually under 25 years old and may not speak fluent English.

Babysitter

Will come to your house and look after the children for a few hours, day or night.

Childminder

Self-employed person who looks after children up to 12 years old in their own home. Childminders must be registered with the Office for Standards in Education, Children's Services and Skills (Ofsted), the government's regulatory body. (gov.uk search ofsted)

Crèche

Provides occasional care for children under 8. Often attached to gyms, yoga studios, shopping centres, churches etc. Some crèches also operate on a stand-alone basis for pre-booked or drop-in hours.

Mother's helper

A non-professional who will do housework and care for children either full or part-time.

Nanny

Provides childcare in your own home. Generally does not do housework or meal preparation for the family, but will take care of all the children's needs, including laundry and meal preparation. Can be live in or out. A nanny will be an employee of yours and as such, will require an employment contract. You are also required to pay National Insurance and tax your nanny appropriately. There are companies that can assist with this such as taxingnannies.co.uk and nannytax.co.uk.

Nursery

Day nurseries and nursery schools provide care for children, usually up to the age of 5. Nurseries are often integrated with early education and are registered with Ofsted. Day nurseries usually care for children from 3 months old, whereas nursery schools often enrol children from the age of 2.

Agencies for childcare

When working with an agency, make sure that you have a complete understanding of the fees charged. There are membership fees, engagement fees and booking fees depending on the situation and agency. These fees vary widely. It is advisable to contact more than one agency. Finding a good match for your specific needs will depend on the sort of people a given agency has on its books at the time you call. Help can be found to suit most permanent and part-time requirements.

Below is a short list of agencies:

- Emergency Childcare: emergencychildcare.co.uk

- The Nanny Service: nannyservice.co.uk

- Sitters: sitters.co.uk

In addition to the agencies listed above, these online resources can be helpful:

- Nannyshare: nannyshare.co.uk

  o Puts you in touch with other local parents so that you can share the cost of a nanny.

- Local Facebook groups can also be a great source of information and connection for parents.

However, these are often private groups for which you need an invitation from another member.

SHOPPING AND SERVICES

All-rounders

These stores and services offer pretty much everything for babies, children and mums-to-be including baby and children's clothing and supplies, toys, nursery furniture, pushchairs, linens, home and car safety equipment as well as maternity clothing and other items for new mums.

- Babylist: anitashouse.com

   o Fee-based consultation service offering a large variety of brand-name nursery and baby items at recommended retail prices. They will help you create a list and/or a wish list of complete nursery needs and deliver them all to you at your convenience.

- Harrods: harrods.com

- John Lewis: johnlewis.com

- JoJo Maman Bébé: jojomamanbebe.co.uk

- Mamas & Papas: mamasandpapas.co.uk

- Mothercare: mothercare.com

DID YOU KNOW?

When shopping for baby clothes, it's helpful to remember that generally, British sizes are spot on, European sizes are a tighter fit and American sizes tend to be cut generously. For example, an average-sized 3-month-old baby will usually fit British and American clothes marked as 3 months but will fit European clothes marked as 6 months. It is, therefore, best to buy European baby clothes at least one size up.

Equipment hire, nappy services and household goods delivery

Chelsea Baby Hire: chelseababyhire.com

- Equipment hire and delivery for long or short term including cots, strollers, highchairs and car seats.

If you are looking to acquire second-hand baby items such as pushchairs, highchairs, furniture and clothing visit:

- Local NCT chapter: nct.org.uk (search 'Nearly New' sales)

- Local FARA Kids charity shop: faracharityshops.org

- Gumtree: gumtree.com

- Local Facebook groups often also have buying/selling/giving pages.

LIVING IN LONDON WITH CHILDREN

London truly is a great place to live and raise children. There are dozens of museums, classes, parks, softplay cafes and children's farms to take advantage of. Generally speaking, most mid-range restaurants and cafes have baby-changing facilities and highchairs available.

Entertaining your children

Baby gyms & music classes

- Gymboree: gymboree-uk.com

  o Activity and music classes from birth to 5 years old. Available for parties. Multiple locations.

- The Little Gym: thelittlegym.eu/UK-landing

  o Developmental gymnastics programme for children for 4 months. Summer camps, weekly classes, birthday parties. Multiple locations.

- Tumble Tots: tumbletots.com

  o Active physical play programme for children 6 months to 7 years old. Multiple locations.

- Monkey Music: monkeymusic.co.uk

  o Music and movement classes for children from 3 months to 5 years old. Multiple locations.

City farms

They may live in a city but your kids can experience farmyard animals and learn about where their food comes from at these city farms (visit farmgarden.org.uk for others):

- Freightliners Farm, Sheringham Road, N7: freightlinersfarm.org.uk

  o Five beehives, goats, rabbits, cattle, farmyard birds, garden and cafe.

- Hackney City Farm, 1A Goldsmiths Row, E2: hackneycityfarm.co.uk

  o Pigs, donkey, goats, sheep, calves, chickens, as well as garden and cafe.

- Kentish Town City Farm, 1 Cressfield Close, NW5: ktcityfarm.org.uk

  o Horses, pigs, sheep, goats and farmyard birds. Riding program, garden, pond. Manure available for a donation.

- Deen City Farm, Merton, SW19: deencityfarm.co.uk

  o Horses, pigs, sheep, cows, goats, ducks, chickens, garden, play area and cafe.

Libraries

Your local library in London is well worth an investigative trip. In addition to excellent collections of children's books, many have CD and DVD lending programmes and organised activities for children. Many libraries have story reading and rhyme times for younger children. The library is also a prime source of information on other local happenings for children, especially during the school holidays.

Museums

There are countless museums in and around London of interest to children of all ages. The major museums in London have special activities, exhibits and quizzes during school holidays.

Parks/playgrounds

There are over 80 parks within a seven-mile radius of Hyde Park Corner. Most parks are open dawn until dusk. Royalparks.org.uk can provide up-to-date listings of activities and events being held in some of London's most popular parks.

Some parks that are especially good for children are:

- Battersea Park, Albert Bridge Road, SW11: batterseapark.org

  o Children's zoo, toddlers' playground and an adventure playground.

- Coram's Fields, 93 Guilford Street, WC1

  o This inner-city playground has an under-5s' sand- and water-themed play area, small animal enclosure, paddling pool and adventure play area for children aged 5 and up.

- Hampstead Heath, Parliament hill, NW3, hampsteadheath.net

  o Swimming pool (the Lido), adventure playground (ages 8+), wading pool and children's playground (near Parliament Hill). Visit the website for 8 special events and a map.

- Golders Hill Park, North End Road, NW11, Within Hampstead Heath.

  o Playground and small zoo.

- Holland Park, Ilchester place, W8

  o Lovely children's play area on the southwestern side of the park has sand, swings and other equipment for the under-8s. Adventure playground for older children.

- Regent's Park, NW1

  o Has three gated children's play areas, paddling and row boats, and at the northern end of the park you will find London Zoo (which also contains a playground).

- Primrose Hill, Prince Albert Road, NW8, Just north of Regent's Park.

  o Has a gated children's play area at the southern end of the park, bordering Prince Albert Road.

- Diana, Princess of Wales Memorial Playground, Kensington Gardens, W8 o Large gated play area on the north side of Kensington Gardens for children up to 12 years old. Sand, swings, slides and lots of wooden play pieces, including a pirate ship.

Restaurants

There are a surprising number of London restaurants that welcome children. Sunday lunch is a popular family meal, so children are usually expected anywhere. Here is a small selection of child-friendly restaurants where you will always find a highchair and baby changing facilities.

- Byron Burger: byronhamburgers.com

  o Excellent burgers with children's menu. Multiple locations.

- Carluccio's: carluccios.com

  o Casual Italian restaurant with children's menu. Multiple locations.

- Giraffe: giraffe.net

  o Family friendly for breakfast, lunch and dinner. Eclectic menu. Multiple locations.

- Le Pain Quotidien: lepainquotidien.com

  o Communal tables, delicious organic breads and pastries. Multiple Locations.

- Rossopomodoro: rossopomodoro.co.uk

o   Traditional food and wine of Naples, especially yummy pizza. Multiple locations.

- Pizza Express: pizzaexpress.co.uk

o   Pizza and pasta restaurant with multiple locations. Offers parties as well.

- Wagamama: wagamama.com

o   Asian restaurant where diners eat at communal tables. Multiple locations.

Chapter 9:

Schools

The London area is full of excellent schools. Finding the school that best meets the needs of one's child and family can take considerable time due to the choice available. The decision should involve a number of considerations including your estimated length of time in London, the age and adaptability of your children and the overall impact that a change to the English system might have on the family.

Before making a decision, families should talk to friends and colleagues with children of similar ages. Additionally, families should visit and speak to as many different schools as possible. Education consultants may also be a valuable resource in selecting the right school.

THE BRITISH SCHOOL SYSTEM

Children in the UK must be in full-time education the term after their fifth birthday.

The system can be confusing to a newcomer and may differ from location to location. Within the British school system, schools are generally grouped into two categories: state schools, which are run by the Government, and independent (private) schools, which are privately run and fee-paying. Confusingly, some of the oldest independent (private) schools are also referred to as "public schools".

State schools may also often include religious foundations schools (i.e., the Church of England and Roman Catholic schools).

State schools

As in any country, some state schools outperform independent schools in the same area. Therefore, choosing a state school may be a very viable option. However, places in the top state schools can be competitive. In many instances, matters are even more complicated for incoming families as many state schools restrict registration until a family can prove residence in the relevant catchment area. If you are considering eligibility for a church-based school and utilising a 'church-place', you may be asked to join and attend the church for a period of time before considering a school application.

However, many local church schools will consider previous church attendance so it is worth speaking with the local vicar and headmaster. All of this makes it very difficult to simultaneously co-ordinate housing and schooling.

Finding reliable information regarding a particular school can be difficult but the Office for Standards in Education (Ofsted), an independent organisation that objectively reports the standards and quality of each school, can be a good place to start. You can read each school's Ofsted report on the Ofsted website: ofsted.gov.uk. Nursery school reports are also available.

To enrol your child in a state school, you should contact the school directly as well as the Local Education Authority (LEA) of the borough in which you plan to live. Most boroughs provide guidance documents and contact information online. In addition, the following organisations may also provide helpful advice:

- The British Council: britishcouncil.org
  o An education information service.

- The Department for Children, Schools and Families: dcsf.gov.uk
  o Overall policy setting government department; they supply the telephone number for your LEA.

- Ofsted: ofsted.gov.uk

- GOV.UK, Schools Page: gov.uk/browse/childcare-parenting/schools-education

Independent schools

Independent schools vary in size, facilities and, most importantly, in philosophy towards education. For example, some schools adhere to sections of the National Curriculum, whereas others have abandoned A-levels and now offer the International Baccalaureate (*covered in more detail* in this chapter) or the Cambridge Pre-U.

Entrance into most schools is determined by examination and/or personal interview. Due to the limited number of spaces and high demand, many schools require long advance notice for admission. As a result, many parents register their children at birth. However, incoming parents should not be put off nor should news that there is no place for your child at a particular school discourage you. Gracious determination sometimes pays dividends.

Although only about 7 per cent of students in England attend independent schools, there are over 2,000 to choose from including local day schools and boarding schools. The boarding school tradition is strong in the UK and it is not uncommon for boys to be sent away at age 8 and girls at age 11. Many good schools, both primary and secondary, are single sex. A number of publications and consulting services are around to help you select a day or boarding school.

All independent schools, including American and international schools, are inspected regularly either by the Independent Schools Inspectorate (ISI) (isi.net), an independent body which reports on the standards and quality of Independent Schools, or by Ofsted (ofsted.gov.uk). You can read a copy of each school's report on the respective websites.

DID YOU KNOW?

Independent schools in England are often referred to as public schools. Until 1902, there were no publicly-supported secondary schools in England. Public schools were supported by an endowment, with a governing body, and were available to all members of the public provided they could pay for tuition costs. Private schools were run for private profit. In recent years, all schools formerly called public schools now refer to themselves as independent schools but the national press (and many individuals) still use the term public school when referring to independent schools. In particular, the older, more prestigious, fee-paying schools mentioned in the Public Schools Act of 1868 (Charterhouse, Eton, Harrow, Merchant Taylors', Rugby, Shrewsbury, St. Paul's, Westminster and Winchester) are typically still referred to as public schools.

Publications and resources

- Gabbitas Guide to Independent Schools: gabbitas.co.uk

  o A comprehensive directory of independent schools (pre-prep to senior) with a geographical directory and advertisements.

- The Good Schools Guide: goodschoolsguide.co.uk

  o Completely independent long-standing schools guide with candid, comprehensive reviews.

- Which London School: whichlondonschool.co.uk

  o Published annually. This guide details independent day, boarding, nursery and international schools in London and the South East.

Educational consultants

Educational consultants can prove extremely valuable and helpful in finding a suitable school for your family. The educational consultant will usually arrange for you to receive school prospectuses. Additionally, he or she will typically arrange for visits to the school, possibly accompanying you on the visits, and then assisting you through the admissions process. However, a good educational consultant will not tell you which school to choose – that is a very personal choice.

Independent British schools: ages for nursery, prep, senior and boarding

The school system in the UK can be confusing. The independent (i.e. privately run) school system in particular, has no standard age at which nursery, junior or senior schools begin and end.

In general, nursery schools take children between the ages of 2½ and 5 years, junior schools will take children from age 5 to 11 or 13 and senior school begins at age 11 for girls and age 13 for boys.

State schools are a bit more straightforward. There is pre-school (for the under-5s), primary school (aged 5 to 11 or 13) and secondary school (until graduation at age 18).

The Wikipedia page dedicated to Education in England can be a helpful starting point: wikipedia.org/wiki/Education_in_England.

International, foreign national and American schools

A number of international schools in the London area cater specifically to expatriate children. These schools are experienced in working with students and families making an international transition. While they all classify themselves as international schools, some do specialise in a national curriculum, while others offer a much more international curriculum and many are increasingly adopting the International Baccalaureate (IB) curriculum standards. Some of the schools provide education for students of specific nationalities with classes taught in their native language.

The International Baccalaureate (IB)

The IB programme is a recognised leader in the field of international education known for its Diploma Programme. The IB Diploma Programme for 16- to 19-year-olds (or the last two years of American high school) is widely recognised by universities internationally and highly regarded as a rigorous programme by universities in over 120 countries including the US, Canada and the UK. The IB Diploma is increasingly offered in many top-performing high schools in the US and Canada with students taking IB courses to fulfil requirements for their high school diploma. Some of the International and American Schools in London offer the IB Diploma alongside the American High School Diploma.

The IB Programme also includes the less well-known Middle Years Programme (MYP) for students in grades six through ten, and Primary Years Programme (PYP) for students in grades pre-kindergarten through five. Like the Diploma Programme, the MYP and PYP are increasingly offered in American, Canadian and International Schools around the world, making it very easy for children to transition from one IB school to another. For more information on the IB, visit their website: ibo.org.

LEARNING DIFFICULTIES OR SPECIAL NEEDS

UK law requires that all state schools must do their best to meet a student's special education needs (SEN), sometimes with the help of outside specialists. There are various guides available to parents on this process obtainable from your local education authority (LEA). If this is support that you need, gov.uk is a good starting point for further information. It is advisable to phone any potential independent schools before visiting and sending in an application.

APPLYING TO AMERICAN UNIVERSITIES

If your child has attended English schools through A-level exams and wishes to attend an American university, few English schools will have prepared him or her for the required SAT exams and be able to help select the best university for his or her needs. Whether your child is taking AP or IB courses and wants to attend a UK university, or taking A levels and wants to attend college back in the US, most colleges and universities will list relevant requirements for students coming from each system.

The US-UK Fulbright Commission – Education USA

The US-UK Fulbright Commission (fulbright.org.uk) is a not-for-profit organisation funded by both governments to promote educational exchange between the US and the UK. The Commission offers prestigious awards for postgraduate study and research in the US as well as an Advisory Service. They hold an annual USA College Day fair as well as other events throughout the year to support students, parents and teachers interested in US study.

Uni in the USA (goodschoolsguide.co.uk/university), published by *The Good Schools Guide*, is a handy British guide to US universities written for UK students but very entertaining and useful for American students. Includes irreverent but thorough reviews of selected colleges written by British students telling what each is really like, and comprehensive articles about the entire US application process.

Chapter 10:

Cooking, food and drink

British cooking has experienced a renaissance in recent years. Modern British cooking is decidedly cool. British food personalities dominate not just British airwaves, but are very popular across the pond as well. Jamie Oliver, Nigella Lawson, Nigel Slater and Mary Berry have all contributed to the modern British food movement. Within London it is exceptionally easy to find a plethora of choice both in terms of home-cooking ingredients and when dining out.

GENERAL TIPS

London kitchens are typically small and are often home to not only the oven and dishwasher but also very possibly the washing machine! Space is at a premium so considering how much you need in terms of crockery and cookware may be a good idea before deciding to bring both sets of wedding china for your move. Consider bringing multiple-use items and budget to purchase those with motors (e.g. blenders) when you arrive to avoid electrical compatibility issues.

Cooking scale

One of the first things you will encounter cooking in the UK is that recipes use metric measures rather than imperial. A quick reference guide is included at the end of the chapter. Purchasing a cooking scale is a good investment for a London kitchen!

Oven

British ovens are often smaller than North American ovens so double check your pans will fit. The average oven is 60cm wide. Most flats will have compact or single ovens. Oven temperature is measured in either

Celsius or Gas Mark. An oven thermometer can be helpful, particularly if you're not sure your Gas Mark guidelines are completely accurate.

Reference: which.co.uk, 2019

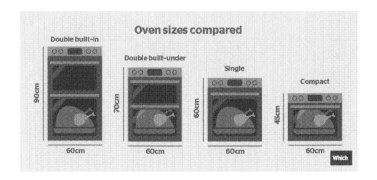

Induction cooking

Induction cooktops, or "hobs", are common in Britain. They create a magnetic field between the induction element in the hob and the pan. As the pan heats up, the cooking surface does not so they are more energy efficient and quicker. Special pots and pans are needed for these hobs. Induction cookware will also work on other cooking surfaces. To check if your pans will work, hold a magnet next to the base. If it attracts, the pan will work on induction.

Water kettle

Electric water kettles are commonplace in British

kitchen. It heats water quickly without using the hob. Purchase second-hand or new when you arrive.

Drinking water

The quality of tap water is regulated by EC and UK legislation. Bottled mineral water is not required to be as thoroughly and regularly tested as tap water and is more likely to contain higher levels of bacteria. London tap water is very hard and some people may find it unpalatable. Water purifiers are a popular alternative to buying bottled water and range from small activated carbon filters attached to a jug to plumbed-in filter systems.

Limescale

The evidence of hard water may be seen on the inside of your kettle, on showerheads and on other household appliances in the form of limescale. Limescale should be removed periodically with a commercial limescale remover (available at supermarkets) or by using a boiled mixture of one-half cup of white vinegar and one-half cup of water. Remember to rinse appliances well after they have been cleaned. It is always a good idea to empty a kettle after each use to avoid re-boiling water, which can concentrate the hardness. This practice is especially important when using boiled water to make baby formula.

FOOD FACTS

Cooking and baking in the UK is easy once you know the common terms of goods available. Bookmark this page on your phone or tablet, or download and print one of the free (and cute!) printables for easy reference when up to your elbows in flour and butter!

Flour

There are many types of flour available in the UK, but the two most common are plain flour and self-raising flour.

- Plain Flour

    o A soft wheat flour, used for pastry and thickening sauces – most similar to American 'all-purpose flour'.

- Self-raising flour

    o Raising agents are already included and do not need to be added for the baking process.

Should you wish to substitute one for the other, it is suggested that you research the appropriate substitutions.

DID YOU KNOW?

Bicarbonate of soda is called baking soda.

Sugar

The British have several varieties of sugar, some of which are better to cook with than others. Here is a description of the most common types of sugar found in supermarkets:

- Caster sugar
  - A fine granulated sugar that dissolves easily and is ideal for baking or desserts.
- Demerara sugar
  - A coarse, crunchy, brown sugar. It is good in coffee or over cereals but is not a substitute for brown sugar in baking.
- Icing sugar
  - Also known as confectioners or powdered sugar.
- Muscovado sugar
  - A soft, dark sugar used in cooking fruit cakes, baked bean casseroles and barbeque sauces. Soft, light and used mainly in baking.

DID YOU KNOW?

The American generic term derived from the brand name Jello is called jelly in the UK because it comes in a concentrated gel. It may not work as a substitute in North American recipes and other baking.

Chocolate

Most cooking chocolate comes in one of three basic forms:

- Bitter
  - A dark bittersweet chocolate used for rich icings and cakes and as a covering for sweets.
- Plain
  - Similar to semi-sweet chocolate.
- Cake covering chocolate
  - Chocolate icing or frosting.

DID YOU KNOW?

It is difficult to locate unsweetened chocolate in the UK. Speciality shops such as Selfridges, Harrods, Partridges, Whole Foods or Fortnum & Mason may carry it but it will be expensive.

For recipes requiring unsweetened chocolate, substitute 3½ tablespoons of unsweetened cocoa plus 1 tablespoon of butter or margarine to equal a one-ounce square of unsweetened chocolate.

Milk

Milk can be purchased in supermarkets and grocers' shops or it can be delivered to your door in plastic containers or returnable glass bottles that are all one size: an Imperial pint (20 ounces).

To arrange milk delivery in your area, check delivermilk.co.uk. All milk in the UK is pasteurised but not all types are homogenised so check the label if that is a concern.

Cream

- Half cream
  - Used like American half and half.
- Single cream
  - 18% butterfat, slightly thicker than half cream.
- Double cream
  - 48% butterfat. Poured over fruits and desserts. Can be whipped but if whipped too much, double cream turns to butter.
- Soured cream
  - 18% butterfat.
- Crème fraiche:
  - 39% butterfat. Also comes in a half-fat version. Similar to sour cream but slightly thicker and less acidic.
- Spooning cream:
  - 30% butterfat. Not suitable for coffee or whipping. Spoon over fruit and desserts.
- Whipping cream:
  - 40% butter fat. Suitable for recipes that require heavy or whipping cream.
- Clotted cream:
  - A speciality from the West of England. Very thick. Used on fruits and desserts and on scones for cream teas.
- Fromage frais:
  - A lightly whipped, lower-fat equivalent of double cream that can be used when cooking. Fruit flavoured fromage frais is a good source of

calcium and is often given as a snack to children in place of yoghurt.

Cheese

English cheeses range from Gloucester (pronounced GLOS-ter), which is mild, to Blue Stilton, which is blue-veined and has a strong, sharp flavour. In between these two extremes, there is Lancashire (LANK-a-sheer) which grates easily and is good in cooking, and Leicester (LES-ter) which is similar to Cheddar. English, Scottish and Irish Cheddars are wonderful all-purpose cheeses that range from mild to mature. Danish Havarti can be substituted for Monterey Jack, although Monterey Jack can be found in large and online supermarkets.

Most international cheeses can be found in a good grocery store or speciality cheese shop.

Butter and margarine

Butter and margarine are widely available in several different varieties. Butter is supplied by different dairy regions in the UK, Ireland and Europe and the difference in taste is a matter of personal preference. Margarine made from 100 percent polyunsaturated fats is sold in grocery stores along with butter/margarine blends.

Eggs

Most eggs are brown and are not refrigerated in supermarkets. They do not need refrigeration because they are so fresh – the 'use by' date stamped on each individual egg is the 21st day after the egg was laid. Both free-range and organic eggs are readily available.

Fruits and vegetables

There is a wide and wonderful assortment of fresh fruits and vegetables available all year round in Britain. You are likely to find a good selection at your local grocery store and market. With the increase in popularity of organic produce, you will find areas within larger stores dedicated to these products.

Beef

Most beef is English but Scottish beef is available at most butchers and supermarkets for a higher price and is considered to be of better quality.

A roast, on or off the bone, is called a joint. Ground beef is called mince. Minced steak is the leanest. If you are accustomed to beef from corn-fed cattle, UK beef may taste slightly different as most UK cattle are grass-fed rather than corn-fed. Steaks for grilling are available in several different cuts, the most common being sirloin, fillet (FILL-it), ribeye and rump. For a pot roast, look for topside, silverside or brisket cuts.

Lamb

British spring lamb is a real treat and unsurpassed for taste. A less expensive alternative is frozen New Zealand lamb. Lamb is available in chops, racks, cutlets, leg roasts and shoulders.

Pork

Pork roast as well as chops, tenderloin and spareribs (called American or Chinese spareribs) are all cuts that are easily found in supermarkets. Gammon is one of the best and most expensive of hams. It is uncooked when purchased. York ham is also of high quality.

A wide variety of bacon is available smoked or unsmoked. The most common bacon in the UK is back bacon. Similar to Canadian bacon, it is larger and meatier than streaky/crispy bacon, which is usually thinner and streaked with fat (similar to American bacon). UK sausages (especially breakfast sausages) tend to have a high cereal content and come in many different flavours and varieties.

Poultry

A wide variety of poultry is available, including free-range chicken, local corn-fed chicken and French corn-fed chicken (of which the most famous is from Bresse). In larger supermarkets, you can find turkey, duck and game birds (such as grouse and pheasant in season). If you prefer, ask for grain-fed, free-range or organic chickens.

Fish

Fish (usually cod, haddock or halibut) and chips is one meal that the British made famous. The availability of fresh local fish is never far away – plaice, skate, brill, flounder, sea bass, sea bream, haddock and cod are readily available! The best quality of lemon sole and Dover sole can be purchased after April. Salmon, from Scotland and Ireland, is best in June, July and August.

There is a large range of shellfish available from local fishmongers and specialist food halls, whilst more and more supermarkets now have their own fish and shellfish counters. Look for prawns (shrimp), crabs, mussels, scallops, lobsters, oysters (in season), langoustines, cockles, whelks and winkles. You may find that most prawns are sold cooked because they are imported – raw prawns can be very expensive.

DID YOU KNOW?

When buying fresh fish, look for brightness, prominent eyes and red gills. The fishmonger will scale, clean and fillet a fish if asked.

Department and speciality stores

Department stores offer a large range of foods and products in their food halls. An international assortment can be found at Harrods, Selfridges, Partridges, Whole Foods, Fortnum & Mason and Harvey Nichols. Marks & Spencer Simply Food is unique in that it only carries its own brand of products, including ready-prepared food and meals. Although the food is more expensive in these department store halls, they are wonderful for speciality items, prepared meals, and foreign products. Several offer home delivery and online orders.

Farmers' markets

Farmers' markets provide an opportunity to purchase locally produced food at its freshest, seasonal peak. Almost all of the produce and goods you will find at a farmers' market has been produced, grown, baked or prepared by the individual stallholder, so you are always assured of the quality and freshness of the items. The selection of items available at a farmers' market will vary depending on season and location but you can usually expect to find a good assortment of fruits, vegetables, meat, eggs, dairy products and speciality products such as homemade preserves, breads and cakes that are not typically found in your local supermarket.

The popularity of farmers' markets in this country continues to grow as a means of encouraging consumers to buy local food and thus help support British farmers. There are markets in many different areas of London. For more information or a complete list of locations and schedules, visit the London Farmers' Markets website: lfm.org.uk.

Farms

For the freshest fruit, pick your own. There are several 'pick-your-own' farms around the M25 motorway. It is advisable to ring each farm for directions, opening times and available crops. Additional items like farm fresh eggs, bread and honey may also be available. A day of picking your own fruit and vegetables is a great family outing. Visit: pickyourown.org.

Local purveyors

Do try your local butcher, fishmonger, baker and greengrocer to experience a more personal service and begin to feel part of your neighbourhood. They will be able to help you source difficult to find cuts of meat and speciality ingredients, including Thanksgiving turkeys!

Organic and health food

The Soil Association is the UK's leading campaigning and certification organisation for organic food and farming. They have an excellent website (soilassociation.org) that contains detailed information on all aspects of organic food and farming. The site also includes a complete list of retail outlets in London and throughout the UK that sell organic food products.

Supermarkets

ASDA, Sainsbury's, Tesco, Co-op, Morrison's, Whole Foods, Marks & Spencer and Waitrose all have a large choice of competitively priced supermarkets in Britain, especially London. They offer a wide range of international products and many remain open long hours or 24 hours a day to meet busy consumer lifestyles.

Stores can be incredibly crowded and run out of items late in the day, before a holiday, or on the Saturday before a bank holiday. Few shops have packers or personnel to take your groceries to your car. Plastic carrier bags are charged at 5p per bag by law in an effort to reduce waste and encourage shopper to bring reusable bags. You will often have to bag your own groceries.

Many local purveyors and larger supermarkets offer online shopping and home delivery. In addition to the range of standard grocery items, several also offer a broad selection of wine, flowers, music, books, recipes and gift items. Delivery procedures vary but in most cases, you will be able to specify a one- or two-hour pre-arranged time slot.

Takeout

On the nights you are too tired to cook, it helps to have some restaurant delivery options on hand. Many restaurants do take-away but most do not offer delivery. It is generally best to check online or call your restaurant of choice and ask. There are now a number of apps which have met this demand for delivery including Deliveroo, UberEats and Just Eat, apps which allow you order takeaway from local restaurants.

International foods and specialities

There are several books available (including *The Essential Guide to London's Best Food Shops* by Antonio Carluccio and *Food Lovers' London* by Jenny Linford) that provide detailed listings of markets and speciality food stores located in many areas of London. It may be worth purchasing one to become acquainted with your neighbourhood's offerings or to locate specific ingredients. Additionally, a quick web search will usually bring up local options.

Warehouse Club

Costco (costco.co.uk) sells high-quality, nationally-branded and selected private-label merchandise at low prices to businesses purchasing for commercial use or resale, and to individuals who are members of selected employment groups. Multiple locations.

Off-licences

Liquor stores or wine shops are known as off-licences. These shops are licensed to sell beer, wine and spirits for consumption 'off' the premises. Most supermarkets also sell alcoholic beverages. Additionally, almost every neighbourhood has its own local off-licence incorporated within a small convenience store that sells everything from crisps to deodorant.

MEASUREMENT CONVERSIONS

The best way to approach cooking in a foreign country is to focus on all the marvellous new tastes and ingredients available and not to focus on the few ingredients that cannot be easily or inexpensively obtained. The British weigh their ingredients so purchasing an inexpensive kitchen scale and measuring utensils will simplify cooking with British recipes.

The British are well known for many things but food has traditionally not been high on the list. Modern British cooking, however, is changing that perception as it reflects the diversity of the people who have settled in Britain. Purchase any one of the excellent cookbooks by modern British cooks such as Nigella Lawson, Jamie Oliver or Nigel Slater and you will be pleasantly surprised. Reliable classics include Delia

Smith's *Cookery Course* or Mary Berry's *Complete Cookbook*.

Many British recipes list ingredients in both imperial and metric measurements. If you are not used to these measurements, the conversion tables and a calculator may be among your most important cooking tools.

Liquid measures

Description	UK imperial/metric	US fluid measures
Teaspoon	5 ml	1/6 oz
Dessertspoon *(2 teaspoons)*	10 ml	1/3 oz
Tablespoon *(3 teaspoons)*	15 ml	1/2 oz
Gill	5 oz/ 142 ml	4 oz/ 118 ml
Cup	10 oz/ 284 ml	8 oz/ 236 ml
Pint	20 oz/ 568 ml	16 oz/473 ml

Dry measures

When measuring dry ingredients such as flour or sugar for a British recipe, remember to weigh the items as the ingredients will be listed in ounces or grams. Remember, eight ounces of two different ingredients may have distinctly different volumes!

Ingredient	UK imperial	UK metric	US imperial
Flour	5 oz	140 g	1 cup
Sugar	1 oz	25 g	2 tbsp
	8 oz	225 g	1 cup
Brown sugar	6 oz	170 g	1 cup
Nuts	4 oz	115 g	1 cup
Yeast	4 oz	7 g	2 tsp
Butter	1 oz	30 g	2 tbsp
	4 oz	113 g	1 stick (8 tbsp)
	8 oz	230 g	1 cup

Further conversions

To convert:	You:
Ounces (oz) to grams (g)	Multiply by 28
Quarts (qt) to litres (l)	Multiply quarts by 0.95
Pounds (lb) to grams (g)	Multiply pounds by 450
Pounds (lb) to kilograms (kg)	Multiply pounds by 0.450
Kilograms (kg) to pounds (lb)	Multiply kilograms by 2.2
Stones to pounds (lb)	Multiply by 14
Centigrade (C) to Fahrenheit (F)	Multiply C by 1.8 and add 32
Fahrenheit (F) to centigrade (F)	Multiply F by 5, subtract 32 and then divide by 9

Cooking temperatures

For fan-assisted ovens, you should either turn the heat down slightly or decrease the cooking time.

Celsius	Fahrenheit	Gas mark	Description
110	225	1	Very slow
125	250	2	Very slow
140	275	2	Slow
150	300	2	Slow
165	325	3	Moderate
180	350	4	Moderate
190	372	5	Moderate/hot
200	400	6	Moderate/hot
220	425	7	Hot
230	450	8	Hot
240	475	9	Very hot

Chapter 11:

Sport and

leisure

Sport and games are an important part of British life. Many sports were invented, developed or unified by the British including golf, skiing, tennis and football. Association football, rugby football and cricket are the most popular. Golf, horse racing, darts, snooker and motorsports also have large followings.

In addition to watching sport, there are also many ways to participate. Your local neighbourhood is a good place to start when looking for a sporting opportunity for yourself or your family.

BRITISH SPORTING TERMINOLOGY

When watching or participating in sport, it is important to know the language. Here are some terms to help you communicate on and off the pitch. These terms will also be used in the following sections.

- Athletics: track and field.

- Cricket: a very popular summer sport. The American sport cricket is most similar to is baseball, however the game play and rules are very different.

- The Derby: pronounced "dar-bee". A famous and prestigious flat horse race held at the Epsom Downs racecourse in Surrey.

- FA Cup: the main football knock-out competition, open to all clubs in England and Wales (amateur and professional).

- Fixture: game, match, contest.

- Football: association football (i.e. soccer) or rugby football but almost exclusively refers to the former. NFL football is known as American football or gridiron.

- Grand National: the world's best-known horse race over fences, run at Aintree, Liverpool, in early April.

- Hockey: field hockey. Ice hockey is known as ice hockey.

- Netball: Predominantly a women's sport. Foundations come from basketball, although the ball is smaller, the ring is smaller and higher and there is no backboard. Seven-player teams.

- The Open: the British open golf championship.

- Pitch: field of play.

- Premiership: an elite league of the best 20 football clubs in England and Wales. There is also a premiership league in rugby union that consists of the top 12 rugby union clubs in the UK. Generally, this term refers to the football league.

- Queen's: Queen's Club Championships (also known as Fever-Tree Championships due to sponsorship reasons) – Prestigious annual men's tennis tournament held at the Queen's Club in West Kensington that serves as a warm-up for Wimbledon.

- Racing/Race Meeting: horse racing.

- Rounders: a version of softball usually played at school.

- Royal Ascot: the world's most famous horse-race meeting, typically held in June. Attended by HM the Queen.

- Rugby: Can refer to either rugby union, which is 15-a-side, or rugby league, which is 13-a-side with a number of different rules. Rugby union has been professional for many years and there are thriving amateur leagues in both.

- Six Nations: premier northern hemisphere rugby union competition between England, Wales, Scotland, Ireland, France and Italy. Usually held in February and March..

- Test Match: an international rugby or cricket match, the latter lasting up to five days.

- Touts: scalpers. Expensive and dubious sources of hard-to-find tickets.

- Wimbledon: one of four grand slam tennis tournaments and the only one played on grass courts. Held annually at the all England club in Wimbledon.

SPECTATOR SPORTS

Tickets to see the biggest sporting events are quite difficult to obtain with the most sought after being Wimbledon (tennis), the FA Cup Final (football), Six Nations fixtures (rugby union), Test cricket matches (cricket) and the Formula One British Grand Prix (motor racing).

Unless you are affiliated with a club, have very good connections or you are prepared to pay vastly inflated prices on the black market, the best way to attend one of these events may be through your employer purchasing a corporate hospitality package or to somehow acquire an invitation to another corporate box or tent.

Regardless of where tickets are found, the best advice is to purchase early!

Football

Football (the word soccer is rarely used) is most popular sport in England and you should try to experience at least one match while living in the UK. The English football league system is a pyramid of leagues interconnected by rules of promotion and regulation. There are two national professional league organisations – the Premier League (top 20 clubs) and the Football League (the original football association for England and Wales which currently represents more than 70 clubs). More information on levels, leagues and ranking systems for both men's and women's football can be found through the Football Association (FA) website: thefa.com.

Season

The official football season runs from August until May, ending with the FA Cup Final. FA Cup finals are normally played at Wembley Stadium.

Premier League

Several of the FA Premier League teams are located in London (visit premierleague.com for a current listing). Tickets to see established Premiership teams like Arsenal, Chelsea and Tottenham Hotspur are hard to obtain, particularly for high-profile matches. Other teams' tickets may be easier to get hold of, such as Watford or West Ham United. Most football clubs allow for bookings via telephone or online.

If you cannot find tickets to a Premier League match, try one of the London clubs in the Championship (one tier below the Premier League). It is usually easier to acquire tickets and many times offers a more representative taste of the national game. Tips for going to the match:

- Professional football matches take place on weekends and on weekday evenings. The traditional kick-off times are 15:00 on Saturday, 13:30 and 16:00 on a Sunday and 20:00 during the week. Always be sure to check the day before the match since the time printed on your ticket can change at short notice due to TV schedules and police requests.

- Most football clubs welcome children but book seats in the designated family areas, which will be specially stewarded.

- Expect opposing supporters to be strictly segregated. If ever offered a match ticket, check where the seats are located. Avoid sitting with the away supporters unless you and your family are diehard fans of the away team. Equally, you may be asked to leave by the stewards if you are seen to be supporting the away team in a home area.

- Take public transport to the game if at all possible. Roads around the ground may be blocked and parking may be virtually impossible.

- Do not try to take food or drink with you as it will probably be confiscated. Not only do clubs prefer you to buy food from the concession stands, cans and bottles are regarded as a safety hazard. Beer is available inside the stadium before and during the match, but cannot be taken to your seat. This applies to corporate boxes as well.

• Dress warmly. Unless in a corporate box, there will be no heating and seats may not be under cover. Matches are usually played rain or shine.

• All stadiums are non-smoking.

Rugby

There are two types of rugby played in England – rugby union (15-a-side) and rugby league (13-a-side). There are various national and international leagues and competitions for both sports. Visit englandrugby.com (rugby union) or superleague.co.uk (rugby league) for more details.

In London and the south, rugby union is far more popular than rugby league. The English national team plays at Twickenham in West London, where Test Matches are played. There is also a Premiership league in which the top 12 professional teams compete. In general, rugby matches have a more relaxed and friendly atmosphere than football matches and opposing supporters are not separated. Tailgate parties in the car park before and after matches are a long-standing Twickenham tradition.

Season

The Six Nations tournament, held in February/March, is the premier northern hemisphere rugby union competition contested between the national teams of England, Wales, Scotland, Ireland, France and Italy. Twickenham hosts the three home matches in this tournament for the England team.

Tickets for Twickenham are notoriously hard to obtain for matches against Australia, New Zealand, South Africa and the Six Nations competition. For those games, unless you are a playing or coaching member of a rugby club, your best bet is to book a hospitality package which will include a ticket, lunch, tea and drinks. These are not cheap and most are bought for corporate entertainment.

If you would like to see a domestic rugby union match, there are several professional clubs based in and around London with Saracens (saracens.com) in Hendon and Harlequins (quins.co.uk), down the road from Twickenham, among the most recognisable. Tickets are relatively easy to obtain except for certain Premiership matches.

Tennis

Tennis is a very old sport in the UK and there are hundreds of local clubs. Grass courts (lawn tennis) are common with many tournaments throughout the year to attend. The Lawn Tennis Association website (lta.org.uk) is the best place to go to find a schedule of tournaments and ticket links. Remember, book early!

Wimbledon

All England Lawn Tennis and Croquet Club (AELTC) is home to the Wimbledon Tennis Championship, the grass court "Grand Slam" tournament. Wimbledon lasts a fortnight (2 weeks) from the start of July. Qualifying tournaments are also held in the area where you can see major men's and women's players.

Catering at Wimbledon is excellent and can be expensive. Cafes serving traditional strawberries and cream along with other items are available within the grounds but you can also take your own picnic (check Wimbledon website for restrictions). There is a large grassy picnic area colloquially known, among other names, as Henman Hill with a big screen relaying live action from Centre Court, Court 1 and Court 2 (also known as the Show Courts).

Set a reminder in August to check the Wimbledon website for tournament ticket information. Ways to attend:

- Submit an application into the UK public ballot for a pair of show court tickets. Tickets are awarded randomly to applicants; submitting an application does not guarantee tickets. Days and courts are randomly assigned, so it is not possible to specify a choice with this method. These cannot be resold or gifted to another person.

- There are special ballot options for schools, coaches and members associated with the Lawn Tennis Association.

- A limited number of Grounds tickets (and sometimes show court tickets!) are available each day to those in the queue. Queues can be very long. Expect to queue overnight for show court tickets or several hours before the grounds open.

- Choose to visit Wimbledon in the late afternoon/early evening, when show court tickets are resold at a lower price for charity once their original holders have left for the day. If you waited in the queue and are on the grounds, you may also purchase these.

Grounds tours are also available year-round. Visit wimbledon.com for the most updated information regarding tickets and to schedule a tour.

Equestrian

Equestrian events are very popular in London and the calendar is packed throughout the year. Here are the top ones not to be missed.

Cheltenham National Hunt Festival

The most important jump racing meeting on the calendar occurs at Cheltenham Racecourse each March. The National Hunt Festival, a combination of steeplechase and hurdle racing, features four major Championship races (in addition to Grade 1 contests and Handicap races) over the course of four days, culminating with the Cheltenham Gold Cup race. Apply for tickets and book accommodation from 30 September. A discount scheme is offered for early purchases:

thejockeyclub.co/uk/cheltenham.

Grand National

The Grand National, held at Aintree Racecourse in Liverpool each April, is perhaps the most famous steeplechase in the world: a four-and-a-half mile race over 30 challenging fences. Tickets are relatively inexpensive and plentiful: thejockeyclub.co.uk/aintree.

Royal Ascot

Race meetings are held at Ascot Racecourse in Berkshire throughout the year – jump racing in the winter and flat racing in the summer. Royal Ascot, held in June, is perhaps the most famous meeting. The Queen, who is an avid horse owner, always attends. Foreign nationals may obtain tickets for the Royal Enclosure at Royal Ascot by application to their embassy or high commission. Morning dress, smart dress or national dress for men, and hats and skirts for ladies must be worn: ascot.co.uk.

The Derby

The Derby, a classic flat race for three-year-old horses, is run every June at Epsom Downs Racecourse in Surrey. This race is a tradition that dates back to 1779: thejockeyclub.co.uk/epsom.

Cricket

Cricket is the English summer national game and is famously said to be incomprehensible to foreigners. However, it is easy to follow once the basic terms are understood. Many believe that there is nothing more peaceful than spending an afternoon beside a village cricket green lounging on a picnic rug, reading the weekend papers and sipping a cup of tea or glass of wine. 20/20 cricket – often abbreviated to T20 – is the shortest form of cricket with each side batting for 20 overs.

You can experience the excitement and atmosphere of a one-day international (50 overs per side) or a five-day Test Match at either Lord's Cricket Ground, St. John's Wood (lords.org) or the Oval Cricket Ground, Kennington (kiaoval.com). Visit England & Wales Cricket Board (ecb.co.uk) for additional information, fixtures and tickets.

Motor racing

The Formula One (F1) British Grand Prix is held in July

at the Silverstone Circuit in Northamptonshire, located 115 km north of London (silverstone.co.uk). The track website provides the full calendar of British motor races for the year.

Moto GP (motogp.com) motorcycle races also take place in the UK during the summer months.

Golf

There are more than 2,500 golf courses in the UK and its popularity has increased dramatically with worldwide TV coverage. Many old, established member-only clubs now allow pay and play on weekdays and some weekends. Strict club rules and etiquette must be observed. The biggest annual golf event is the Open Championship, which is rotated around links (seaside) courses in England and Scotland. You will need to book in early spring for general admission tickets: britishopengolf.com.

PARTICIPATING IN SPORT

Sport England outlines the government's sporting objectives in the UK. It works through nine regional offices that can provide information on sporting activities throughout England. Visit the website to research sport opportunities in a specific area: sportengland.org.

Public facilities

Most boroughs have public recreational and leisure facilities such as pools, tennis courts, classes and parks. Some councils run a residents' discount scheme which entitles members to reductions on certain gym memberships and other activities. Each council has its own public sports and leisure centres which can be found on the council's website. A full listing of councils can be found on: local.gov.uk (search local councils).

Private health clubs and gyms

London health clubs and gyms are generally expensive to join and often demand a guarantee of at least one year's commitment. Before joining, ask for at least a fortnight's trial and shop around to find the right one for you. Check your local residents' magazine or newspaper for the most up-to-date information on new club openings in your area.

Golf

There are a few golf courses in central London and some hidden driving ranges. Do not expect golf carts as they are rare in the UK. For more information on courses in the London area and information about clubs, visit The English Golf Union: englandgolf.org.

Note that at traditional golf clubs, shirts with collars

are obligatory for everyone and ladies' shorts should be at knee length. Some clubs also require men to wear knee-high socks with shorts. Ask your host beforehand if in doubt.

Horse riding

London's green spaces make it an ideal city for horse riding and this remains an active pastime of the Royal Family. There are stables all across London where you can hire equipment, usually for a small fee. Helmets are compulsory in the UK. Most stables require children to be at least four or five years of age to ride.

Ice hockey

The Ice Hockey UK website provides information on non-professional UK ice hockey leagues (e.g. women's teams, juniors or recreational play): icehockeyuk.co.uk.

Ice skating

For the winter holiday period (late November – early January), a number of venues throughout London will set up ice rinks. Notable are Somerset House, Broadgate Ice Rink (near Liverpool Street station), the Natural History Museum, Hampstead Heath, the Tower of London, Hampton Court Palace and Kew Gardens.

Rowing

There are many boat clubs along the Thames that train and compete in crews for regattas and head races. The most famous are the Henley Royal Regatta in Oxfordshire, held in July, and the Head of the River Race on the Thames in March. Most also have active social programmes and are an excellent way to meet people.

Rugby

Men's, women's and mixed touch rugby leagues of various levels compete at venues in and around London. Emphasis is on the social aspects of the game. Individuals may sign up to be placed on a team. Visit in2touch.com/england to learn more about the various leagues and venues.

Running

London is a great city to run in and local council gyms and leisure centres often organise running clubs for members. Besides the famous London Marathon, there are many races across the year to participate in, ranging from 5K to half-marathons in various parts of the city.

Swimming

Your local council provides a list of local public pools and/or leisure centres. Some councils offer free pool access to those under 16 and over 60. A list of all swimming pools and their facilities in greater London may be obtained from londonswimming.org. During the warmer summer months, London has several lidos (outdoor swimming pools) including the Serpentine Lido in Hyde Park, Brockwell Park Lido in Herne Hill and the Parliament Hill Lido in Hampstead Heath.

Walking and hiking

The Inner London Ramblers Association (ILRA) runs regular free, guided walks on the weekends in the London area. The walks are five to six miles long and start and finish at public transport points within Travelcard zones. (londonramblers.org.uk)

Within one hour from central London by train or car, you can walk in beautiful countryside on many public footpaths and trails. Two easily accessible trails by train are the North Downs Way National Trail in Kent (nationaltrail.co.uk) and the 1066 Country Walk in Sussex (visit1066country.com).

ROYAL PARKS

The Royal Parks (royalparks.gov.uk) look after eight parks throughout London owned by the Crown. These include:

- Bushy Park: 450 hectares/1,099 acres lying north of Hampton Court Palace

  o Contains the famous Chestnut Avenue with its Arethusa 'Diana' Fountain.

- Green Park: 16 hectares/350 acres

  o A peaceful refuge, popular for sunbathing and picnics in good weather. Paths used by runners.

- Greenwich Park: 73 hectares/183 acres

  o Views of the Thames, Docklands and the City of London from its hilltop. Contains the Old Royal Observatory, the Royal Naval College, the National Maritime Museum and the Queen's House. Sanctuary for deer, foxes and birds.

- Hyde Park: 140 hectares/350 acres

  o Provide facilities for many different leisure activities and sports as well as being a focal point for public events of all sizes. Contains the Diana, Princess of Wales Memorial Fountain.

- Kensington Gardens: 111 hectares/275 acres adjacent to Hyde Park

  o Contains Kensington Palace and the Diana, Princess of Wales Memorial Playground. Popular with sunbathers and runners. Cycling is permitted on designated paths.

- Regent's Park: 197 hectares/487 acres

  o Largest outdoor sports area in London. Also contains the Open Air Theatre (home of the New Shakespeare Company in the summer), London Zoo and many cafes and restaurants.

- Richmond Park: Largest open space in London (1,000 hectares/2,500 acres)

  o Home to an important array of wildlife. Varied landscape of hills, woodland gardens and grasslands. Popular for cycling on unpaved terrain.

- St. James's Park: 144 hectares/360 acres of parkland

  o Located in the heart of London, bordered by three royal palaces. Live concerts twice a day in the summer. Children's playground, cafe.

COMMUNITY PARKS

Most community parks are open from dawn until dusk. Notable community parks include:

- Alexandra Park and Palace: 80 hectare/200 acre public park surrounding a palace.

  o Has sporting facilities (including an ice rink) and plenty of attractions for children including a playground, boating lake and small animal enclosure. Children's shows and workshops in the summer. Nature reserve with woodlands, dense scrub, meadow and pond. The Parkland Walk is a shady walk that follows an old rail bed.

- Battersea Park: 83 hectare/200 acre park bordered on one side by the Thames River.

  o Contains a boating lake, children's zoo, deer park, playground, Old English Garden, tree and nature trails, the Peace Pagoda and a herb garden.

- Crystal Palace Park: 140 hectare/350 acre park.

  o Boating and bands during the summer. The maze, farmyard, lake and play area are all popular with children.

- Golders Hill Park: 63 hectare/159 acre area within Hampstead Heath.

  o Playground and small zoo (deer, goats, ducks, etc), putting green, good cafe and beautiful gardens.

- Hampstead Heath: 316 hectares/791 acres.

  o Ponds, woodlands, trails and museums. Famous for kite flying on Parliament Hill with a beautiful view of central London. Swimming ponds, swimming pool, wading pool, tennis courts, concerts in summer at Kenwood House, cafes, playgrounds, animal enclosures, horseback riding, cycling, walking paths and more.

- Highgate Woods: 28 hectares/70 acres.

  o Shady woodland, including an adventure playground, nature hut and trails, and a vegetarian cafe.

- Holland Park: 21 hectares/52 acres.

○ Kyoto Japanese Garden, rose gardens, abundant wildlife, an ecology centre, a wildlife pond, tennis courts, golf driving range and an adventure playground. There is an open air theatre and opera in the summer against the backdrop of Holland House.

- Queen Elizabeth Olympic Park: 560 acre park.

○ Urban park built for the 2012 Olympic games plus waterways, playgrounds, cafes.

- Primrose Hill: 24 hectares/61 acres of grassy hill.

○ Includes a children's playground and outdoor gymnasium. Fantastic views of London.

- Royal Botanic Gardens, Kew: 120 hectares/300 acres

○ Lake, an aquatic garden, a pagoda, Kew Palace and Palm House, among many other things. A World Heritage Site.

Water activities

The mighty River Thames flows over 210 miles from the heart of the Cotswolds through the centre of London and out into the North Sea. Besides its natural beauty, it provides numerous fun outdoor activities including rowing, sailing, punting, kayaking and canoeing and walking along the 184-mile Thames Path: visitthames.co.uk.

Chapter 12:

Culture and

tradition

London provides diverse cultural opportunities ranging from museums, art galleries, historic homes, parks and gardens, to a broad spectrum of performing arts. Experiencing the culture of London also means understanding traditions, local language and perhaps hosting your own high tea or Sunday dinner.

PUBS AND RESTAURANTS

Pub culture

Pubs in England have been around almost 2,000 years and London is home to over 3,000 of them.

They say that if you want to understand the locals, you should head to your nearest pub where you can converse with others and get to know the area around you. If you find yourself at the bar, know you are open to conversations with your fellow pub mate!

If you find yourself visiting a pub on a Sunday, in all likelihood they will be serving a traditional Sunday roast (roast meat with various sides) so do experience this very British tradition!

Types of pubs

Country pub

This is a rural public house found in a village or other rural community.

Theme pubs

These pubs serve niche customers such as sports fans, rock fans and certain nationalities (e.g. Irish pubs).

Gastro pub

A pub that serves high-quality food.

3 Historic London pubs to consider visiting:

The Spaniards Inn

Based in Hampstead, this charming pub has seen the literary likes of Byron, Keats, and Dickens pass through its doors back in the day:

thespaniardshampstead.co.uk.

Ye Ole Cheshire Cheese

Located in the City of London, this local legend has been a favourite of many through the ages including PG Wodehouse and Dickens (he was a pub aficionado!).

The Footman

One of the oldest pubs in London, it served the footmen who served the households of Mayfair who would often ride ahead of their master's coaches:

thefootmanmayfair.com.

Dress code for pubs

Dress is casual and smart-casual for a gastro pub. As is the case for any dine-in eating establishment in London (and throughout Europe), athletic attire/shoes are usually frowned upon.

MUSEUMS, ART GALLERIES, HISTORIC HOMES

London has publicly- and privately-owned museums, galleries and other landmarks. Many of the public museums do not charge admission except for special exhibitions. Becoming a member gives you special privileges such as easier access to major exhibitions, discounts on entrance fees, restaurants and gift shops and invitations to special functions. Privileges vary – contact the individual institutions directly for information.

It is a good idea to call ahead and/or check the websites of museums and other venues in London before making a visit. Unexpected closures or modification of opening hours occur from time to time without prior notice. London's museums are varied and range from those with a broad, mass appeal, to those with a more specifically defined focus.

PERFORMING ARTS

London benefits from a wide range of venues for the performing arts. An essential guide to what is on offer each week is Time Out London (timeout.com/london), published every Tuesday and available at newsagents. It lists current and upcoming events, locations, dates, times, ticket prices and reviews.

Each venue will have its own plan relating to membership benefits and discounted tickets. Some venues offer concessions for groups such as students, pensioners, union members and residents of certain neighbourhoods (e.g. Westminster, Barbican). Other venues reserve a set number of tickets for same-day sales, often at a discount. Still others offer membership schemes with benefits that include early booking information and ticket discounts. Check with the specific venue to determine what discount schemes they offer either in advance or for same-day performances.

MUSIC

London offers options for every musical taste. World-famous artists as well as newcomers perform regularly at venues large and small. Classical performances can be found across the city. Live music of all sorts is available seven days a week.

The O2 arena is a multi-purpose indoor arena located on the Greenwich peninsula and houses the largest indoor concert venue in London as well as numerous bars and restaurants (theo2.co.uk). Another major concert venue in London is Wembley Arena (ssearena.co.uk). There are many smaller independent venues which attract big name artists as well as newcomers on the London music scene. Check out *Time Out London* or your local papers to see which venues are nearest to you.

THEATRE

London has a vibrant theatre scene and has been a destination for theatre fans since the 1800s! From major musicals to plays, stand-up comedies, children's theatre, circus performances, opera shows and dance performances, there are theatre options for everyone.

The concentration of London theatre venues, particularly the large, commercial ones, are located in London's West End. The weekly listings magazine *Time Out London* (timeout.com/london) provides comprehensive coverage of all London theatre productions. Tickets to most West End shows are available from theatre box offices, ticket agencies (e.g. Ticketmaster), major department stores, hotels and online. Useful reference websites are londontheatre.co.uk and officiallondontheatre.co.uk.

Theatre box offices frequently offer same-day price reductions on standby tickets (either on a limited number of tickets released that morning or for concessions) and returned tickets can often be bought for full price one hour before the show. As a rule, these tickets can be bought from the box office in person only.

Summer in London is a fun time for the theatre scene with several outdoor options. For an overview, see *Chapter 14: Annual events*.

COMEDY

For a thorough list of pubs and clubs that provide stand-up comedy events, visit: comedyonline.co.uk.

DANCE

For a current list of news and events related to ballet and dance in the UK, visit: ballet.org.uk. An acclaimed classical ballet company, featuring British and national talent, tours extensively throughout Europe and presents two high profile seasons at the London Coliseum at Christmas and at Royal Albert Hall in the summer.

OPERA

The English National Opera; London Coliseum, St. Martin's Lane, WC2 (eno.org). The resident opera company presents performances in English.

LIKE A LOCAL

Speaking like a local in the UK does not require learning a new language, even though it may seem like it sometimes. Recognising a few common phrases and words will help minimise confusion.

UK English Term	American English Equivalent
Aubergine	Eggplant
Bangers	Sausages
Bin	Garbage pail
Biscuit	Cookie
Brolly	Umbrella
Bonnet	Hood of auto
Boot	Trunk (storage area of auto)
Buggy	Shopping cart
Car park	Parking lot
Chemist	Drug store
Chips	French fries
Cinema	Movie theatre
Cos (lettuce)	Romaine
Courgette	Zucchini
Crisps	Thin chips or crackers
Current Account	Checking Account
Dickies	Tuxedo front
Dressing Gown	Bathrobe
Fancy Dress	Costume
Financial Year	Fiscal Year
Full Stop (punctuation)	Period
Ground Floor	First Floor
Garden	Backyard, patio
HM	Her Majesty

Jumper	Sweater/sweatshirt
Icing Sugar	Confectioners' Sugar
Lift	Elevator
Loo/Cloakroom/Water Closet (WC)	Restroom/Bathroom/Toilet
Lorry	Truck
Mac	Raincoat
Motorway	Highway/freeway
Pavement	Sidewalk
Petrol	Gasoline
Postbox	Mailbox
Post code	Zip code
Pub	Bar that may or may not serve food
Pudding	Dessert
Queue	Line
Rubbish	Trash
Solicitor	Attorney
Sultanas	Golden raisins
Surgery/Consulting Room	Doctor's office
Sweets	Candy
Hoover	Vacuum
Tangerine	Clementine/Satsuma
Torch	Flashlight
To ring up	To phone
Trolley	Shopping Cart
Tube	Subway/Underground
Wardrobe	Closet

| Wellies | Wellington boots/rain boots |

COMMUNICATION TIPS

The best way to learn is to listen and ask. Ask your colleagues or neighbours for their suggestions. Here a few we find helpful.

- Do not assume everyone identifies as "English". Those that live in Wales identify as "Welsh", Scotland are "Scottish", and London are generally "English".

- Start an interaction with the more formal "hello", rather than "hi", "hey" or "How are you?"

- Casual touching of arms, a hug, etc. is frowned upon.

- Do not say "can I get" when ordering. Instead, say "I will have..." or "May I please have..."

Chapter 13:

British food

traditions

Over the years, the Junior League of London has accumulated an array of British food traditions that we thought our readers might find interesting as well as useful.

So whether you're inviting friends over for a 'cuppa' or trying to better understand the local English customs, we hope you enjoy these as much as we have here in Londontown.

FOR THE LOVE OF TEA: THE QUINTESSENTIAL ENGLISH HIGH TEA

"There are few hours in life more agreeable than the hour dedicated to the ceremony known as afternoon tea."

– Henry James

Types of afternoon tea

In general, there are 5 types of tea occasions in England.

Afternoon tea

Served between 3-4pm. This tea used to be served on low tables and is sometimes referred to as "low tea". Historically it was reserved for the upper classes to bridge the gap between lunch and dinner.

The English Afternoon tea usually consists of sweet bites (pastries), savoury bites (finger sandwiches) and scones served with clotted cream and jam. And don't forget the pot of tea!

High Tea

Originally the High Tea was something that was created by the working class as they operated on a different schedule and budget. After a long, gruelling day in the factory, they came home famished and wanting something hearty and substantial. The High Tea comprised of tea, veggies, potatoes, cheese and sometimes meat.

High Tea is often confused with Afternoon tea and is used to lure tourists in London thinking that it's a 'fancier' tea.

Cream Tea

This Tea is only one course (scones with clotted cream).

Royale Tea

This Tea is typically for a more celebratory or special occasion – add champagne or sherry. Cheers!

Builder's Tea

Builder's tea is the English colloquial term for a strong, inexpensive cup of tea typically drunk by construction workers on a break.

How to make "proper" English Tea

Making proper English tea is more art than science.

The kettle

Tea in England is made with tea kettles (usually electric). Most expats who move to London are surprised when they find their microwaved tea to be met with aghast by their English friends. Tea brewed in the microwave tastes different than when brewed with electric tea kettles. The kettle can provide a more even temperature for the tea. You will be pleasantly surprised how much better tea tastes when brewed using a kettle.

Do not re-boil the water in the kettle. Many of us are guilty of this! Re-boiling the water in the kettle will give you a flat tea as the water loses all the oxygen. To avoid this, use fresh clean water every time.

Making tea

Once your kettle is boiling with fresh water you need to leave it for a few minutes to cool down. Otherwise the boiling water will burn the tea.

- Once your water has rested for about 2 minutes, pour into the tea.
- Brew tea for around 3 minutes or according to the directions. Loose leaf tea takes a little longer to brew. Brew longer for a stronger cup of tea.
- Add milk. Whether you add it in at first or after the tea has steeped is entirely debateable.
- Sugar is optional.

AFTERNOON TEA RECIPES

Below is a selection of recipes to serve for an English Afternoon Tea. Enjoy!

Scones with strawberries and clotted cream

Ingredients

50g butter (unsalted)

200g self-raising white flour

1 tbsp white caster sugar

Salt

125ml milk (whole)

Directions

1. Preheat the oven to 220°C (200°C fan) and line a baking sheet with parchment paper.

2. Rub the butter into the flour until the mixture resembles breadcrumbs. Stir in the sugar and salt.

3. Make a well in the centre of the mix and stir in milk. Stir until the mixture is even and the dough comes together.

4. Turn out onto a floured surface and shape into a rough square about 3-4cm thick. Transfer to the prepared baking sheet.

5. Brush all over with milk and cut into rough squares.

Bake for 15 minutes until golden and cooked through. Cool on a wire rack. Serve warm or cold, plain or with jam and cream.

Serve with freshly cut strawberries and clotted cream (e.g. Rodda's Cornish Clotted Cream)

Source: Allrecipes: Paul's Basic Scones

Tea sandwiches

An afternoon tea is served with 3-4 sandwiches cut into small bite-sized pieces.

Egg & Mayo

Ingredients
8 slices of white bread
80g butter
4 free-range eggs, hard boiled, chopped

2 tbsp mayonnaise

Romaine lettuce

Directions

1. Cook the eggs in boiling water for 8 minutes.
2. Spread the bread slices with butter or vegetable spread.
3. In a bowl, mix the chopped hard-boiled eggs with the mayonnaise, then spread on 4 of the bread slices.
4. Top with lettuce hearts and the remaining bread, then   cut into quarters.

Cucumber & Mint

Ingredients

8 small slices wholemeal bread

¼ to ½ tub cream cheese

1 heaped tsp mint jelly

20 slices cucumber

Margarine or butter spread

Directions

1. In a bowl combine the cream cheese and mint jelly.
2. Butter the bread and remove crusts. Lay 5 slices of cucumber on each 4 bread halves. On the other 4, spread the cream cheese mixture. Close to form a sandwich and cut in half. Repeat with remaining and serve.

Tuna

Ingredients

6 or 8 slices brown bread

Butter

170g tin of tuna in water, drained

1 ½ tbsp mayonnaise

½ tbsp salad cream

½ teaspoon lemon juice

Fresh ground black pepper

Directions

1. Combine the tuna, mayonnaise, salad cream, lemon juice and pepper, taking care to retain some of the tuna in chunks.
2. Spread the butter on the slices of bread.
3. Spread the tuna mixture over half of the slices. I use between 1 ½ and 2 tablespoons of tuna mixture per round of bread.
4. Lay some cucumber slices on top if you wish. Put the slices together, trim off the crusts, and cut into triangles, squares or fingers.

Source: Sainsbury's, AllRecipes

Victoria Sponge Cake

Popular during the reign of Queen Victoria, who was known to delight in a slice of sponge cake with her afternoon tea.

Ingredients

200g unsalted butter, softened, plus extra for greasing

200g caster sugar

1 tsp vanilla extract

4 medium eggs

200g self-raising flour, plus extra for dusting

About 6 tbsp raspberry jam

250ml double cream, whipped

Icing sugar for dusting

Directions

1. Heat oven to 190°C/170°C fan. Grease and flour two 20cm sandwich tins

2. Place 200g softened unsalted butter, 200g caster sugar and 1 tsp vanilla extract into a bowl and beat well to a creamy consistency.

3. Slowly beat in 4 medium eggs, one by one, then fold in 200g self-raising flour and mix well.

4. Divide the mix between the cake tins, place into the oven and bake for about 20 mins until risen and golden brown. The cakes should spring back when gently pushed in the middle.

5. When ready, remove from the oven and allow to cool for 5 mins in the tin before turning out onto a wire rack and cooling completely.

6. Spread about 6 tbsp raspberry jam onto one cake and top with 250ml whipped double cream. Sandwich the cakes together and dust with icing sugar.

Source: BBC GoodFood

FULL ENGLISH BREAKFAST

"And then to breakfast, with what appetite you have."

– Shakespeare

The Full English Breakfast is perhaps one of the most recognised breakfasts in the world. Winston Churchill was known to start his busy day with a full English in bed, polished off with a with a cigar and whisky. A traditional Full English Breakfast consists of bacon, eggs, British sausage, baked beans, fried tomatoes, mushrooms, black pudding and toast.

PANCAKE TUESDAY & PANCAKE RACES

Pancake Day, or Shrove Tuesday, is the day in February or March immediately preceding Ash Wednesday when Pancakes are traditionally eaten. In the UK, pancake races form an important part of the Shrove Tuesday celebrations – people often dress up in fancy dress to race down streets flipping pancakes whilst carrying a frying pan.

IS IT PIMM'S O'CLOCK YET?

Pimm's is the British summertime liqueur made of fruits and serves as the official tipple of Wimbledon.

Ingredients

200ml Pimm's No. 1

600ml lemonade

Garnish with mint sprigs and sliced cucumber or mint sprigs with sliced oranges and strawberries.

Directions

Fill a jug with ice and pour over the Pimm's and lemonade. Stir and add the mint, cucumber and fruit.

CHRISTMAS

Markets and tables are stocked with mulled wine and mince pies during the holidays. Whilst regular red and white wine are drunk a lot in Britain, mulled wine is specifically British. Mulled wine is traditionally served at Christmas and is hugely popular here.

Mulled wine

Ingredients

½ bottle red wine

1 cinnamon stick

2 star anise

2 cloves

1 orange, sliced

1 lemon, sliced

50g brown sugar

Directions

1. Place all of the ingredients into a saucepan and simmer gently for 6-8 minutes without boiling. Alternatively, place the ingredients in your slow cooker and cook on low until warm (1-2 hours, depending on your slow cooker).

2. To serve, pour the mulled wine into heatproof glasses.

Mince pies

During the Stuart and Georgian times in the UK, mince pies were filled with meats and were considered a status symbol at Christmas. Today, they are often featured with holiday drinks and are filled with currents, sultanas, candied peel and apples.

Ingredients

350g high-quality mincemeat

225g plain flour

2 tbsp caster sugar

125g unsalted butter, diced

1 large egg, beaten

Milk to glaze

Directions

1. Lightly butter a 12-case patty tin. Tip the mincemeat into a bowl and stir so that the liquid is evenly distributed.

2. Place the flour, sugar and butter in a food processor and process briefly until resembling breadcrumbs, then slowly add the egg through the feeder tube (or rub the butter into the dry ingredients by hand and stir in the egg).

3. Bring the mixture together with your hands, wrap in cling film and chill for an hour. Thinly roll out the pastry onto a floured surface. Cut out 12 circles with a fluted pastry cutter large enough to fill the cases in the patty tin. Press gently into each case, then fill evenly with the mincemeat.

4. Cut out another 12 slightly smaller circles and use to cover the mincemeat. Press the edges together with the end of a fork to seal. Make a small slit in the top of each, then brush lightly with milk. Chill for about 30 mins.

5. While chilling, preheat the oven to 200°C Bake the pies for 20 minutes until golden brown. Cool on a wire rack and serve warm.

Source: BBC GoodFood, AllRecipes

THE SUNDAY ROAST

One of England's oldest culinary traditions, the Sunday Roast can be traced back to Henry VII and his Yeoman (Royal Bodyguard). One in particular was called "beefeater" because of his love of eating roast beef.

Throughout the industrial ages, every household would place a roast in the oven before heading to church every Sunday. Upon their return, the meat was cooked and ready for their dinner. Even now, every Sunday thousands of British families sit down together to eat a feast of roasted meat served with potatoes, vegetables and other accompaniments.

A VERY BRITISH SUNDAY

The components of a classic British Sunday are:

Sunday papers

Whether you prefer to read The Times, the Guardian, or The Telegraph, London is home to some of the most widely-read newspapers in the world. It's common practice in London to buy a thick bundle of the Sunday papers and pore over them as you drink your coffee at home or in a cafe, often leaving the papers there as a courtesy for the next person, who might enjoy reading them.

Long walk

A leisurely stroll, perhaps through one of London's verdant Royal parks or one further afield to work up a hearty appetite.

Roast

By late afternoon, the family sits down to enjoy a Sunday roast of meat or poultry, vegetables and stuffing.

Downtime

Gearing up for the week ahead, a post-roast nap is not unheard of, or staying cosy indoors during the cold winter months drinking copious amounts of tea. Whatever way you unwind, it's part of the unofficial British Sunday.

Chapter 14:

Annual

events

To assist you in planning an exciting year, here is a month-by-month schedule of events along with advice on when and where to obtain tickets. For those events requiring advance planning and/or ticket purchase, we have added reminders at the time of year when you must send away for tickets.

Do your research before attending an event:

- Dress codes are often in effect. Check with the relevant website before planning.

- For events such as Wimbledon, The Queen's Garden Party, Trooping the Colour and Ascot, tickets must be obtained through a lottery or ballot. Entry forms, referred to as ballots, must be submitted by a designated deadline.

- Individual castles, stately homes and numerous other venues offer their own calendar of events. Websites usually list a detailed schedule.

- HM = Her Majesty

Please Note: The following information is accurate at the time of publication. It is strongly suggested that you always verify details before making your plans. You should either call the venue directly or visit the websites: visitlondon.com or visitbritain.com.

JANUARY

- 1 JANUARY: BANK HOLIDAY, NEW YEAR'S DAY PARADE

o Inaugurated in 1987 as the Lord Mayor of Westminster's annual parade, this parade travels through West End London and includes floats, marching bands, concerts and even a street food village! The parade concludes with a fireworks display in the evening. Tickets through lnydp.com from November.

- 1 JANUARY – 28 FEBRUARY: Submit application for Ballots to Trooping the Colour (May/June).

- 1 JANUARY: Bookings open for Chelsea Flower Show (May), Derby Festival (June) and the Goodwood Festival (July).

- 6 JANUARY: ROYAL EPIPHANY GIFTS SERVICE

o Officers of the Royal Household give gold, frankincense and myrrh in the Chapel Royal at St James's Palace. The gold is changed for coin, which is given to charity. yeomenoftheguard.com\epiphany

- 31 JANUARY: Tickets for Beating the Retreat (June) are available.

- EARLY JANUARY: OPENING OF THE OLD BAILEY

o An ancient ceremony to open the new court session where the Queen's Justices are in full bottomed wigs and the Mayor of London is in his 19th-century robes and ostrich plumed hat. The Lord Mayor leads a procession from Mansion House to Central Criminal Court to open a new session.

- LAST SUNDAY IN JANUARY: SERVICE COMMEMORATING CHARLES I

o Procession from St Martin-in-the-Fields to Trafalgar Square commemorates the anniversary of the execution of Charles I. Wreaths are laid on the statue of Charles I in Trafalgar Square and there is a special service in Whitehall to commemorate the "Royal Martyr". Services are conducted at churches nationwide: skcm.org.

- THROUGHOUT JANUARY: STORE SALES! Most stores have major sales beginning in late December and ending in late January. Though traditionally beginning on Boxing Day, the sales have recently been brought forward due to increased competition.

- THROUGHOUT JANUARY: Application forms available for submitting work (amateur or professional) to the Royal Academy Summer Exhibition (June).

- LATE JANUARY OR EARLY FEBRUARY: CHINESE NEW YEAR CELEBRATIONS

  o London's celebration for the Chinese New Year includes traditional and contemporary Chinese entertainment, fireworks in Leicester Square, cultural stalls, food, decorations and lion dance displays in Chinatown and performance stage with local Chinese artists. This is usually celebrated on the Sunday nearest the date of the New Year.

FEBRUARY

- 6 FEBRUARY: ACCESSION OF HM THE QUEEN

  o Anniversary salute of 41 guns in Hyde Park by the King's Troop of the Royal Horse Artillery and a 62-gun salute at the Tower of London by the Honourable Artillery Company. No tickets required.

- FIRST SUNDAY IN FEBRUARY: CLOWN SERVICE

  o In memory of the famous clown Joseph Grimaldi (1778-1837), clowns gather for a church service at Holy Trinity Church, Beechwood Road, Dalston E8.

The service is attended by many clowns in full costume. No tickets required.

- MID-FEBRUARY: LONDON FASHION WEEK

  o Europe's largest selling exhibition for designer fashion: londonfashionweek.co.uk

- LATE FEBRUARY OR EARLY MARCH (SHROVE TUESDAY): PANCAKE DAY RACE

  o The tradition dates to the time when people emptied their pantries of all ingredients and made pancakes before fasting for Lent. Now races are held in which teams run for the finish line while flipping pancakes in frying pans. These activities take place in virtually every British neighbourhood and town.

MARCH

- 28 MARCH: ORANGES AND LEMONS CHILDREN'S SERVICE

  o A church service of thanks for the restoration of the bells of St. Clement Dane (of nursery rhyme fame). Children of the St. Clement's Dane Primary School receive oranges and lemons.

- SECOND WEEK IN MARCH: RHS LONDON FLOWER SHOW

  o The Royal Horticultural Society's important early flower show featuring spring flora: rhs.org.uk.

- SECOND WEEK OF MARCH: THE AFFORDABLE ART FAIR, BATTERSEA PARK

  o Numerous galleries from around the UK and the world display works from their collections. A great place to browse, buy and learn about art. The event is held bi-annually (the second show is usually in October). A free shuttle runs from Sloane Square to the venue: affordableartfair.com.

- SECOND WEEKEND OF MARCH: YONEX ALL ENGLAND BADMINTON CHAMPIONSHIPS

  o Normally held in the National Indoor Arena in Birmingham: badmintonengland.co.uk.

- SECOND/THIRD WEEK OF MARCH: CHELTENHAM NATIONAL HUNT FESTIVAL, GLOUCESTERSHIRE

  o One of the most important jump racing events of the year with top British and Irish horses competing: thejockeyclub.co.uk/cheltenham.

- MOTHERING SUNDAY – MOTHER'S DAY

  o Mothering Sunday is always the middle Sunday of Lent.

- LAST SUNDAY IN MARCH: BRITISH SUMMER TIME BEGINS

  o Clocks move forward one hour. Daylight savings time in Britain begins a few weeks after North Americans adjust their clocks.

- ASH WEDNESDAY: CAKES AND ALE CEREMONY

  o Members of the Worshipful Company of Stationers (founded in 1403) proceed from Stationers Hall to St Paul's Cathedral, where a special sermon takes place. Cakes and ale are dispensed following the sermon.

- END OF MARCH (USUALLY SATURDAY BEFORE OXBRIDGE BOAT RACE): HEAD OF THE RIVER RACE

  o Rowing competition from Mortlake to Putney in southwest London. It is considered to be the largest continuous rowing event in the world. There is a procession of boats throughout the race. The best view is thought to be from the north side of Hammersmith Bridge: horr.co.uk.

- SATURDAY IN MARCH OR APRIL: OXFORD AND CAMBRIDGE BOAT RACE

  o Held annually since 1829, the race course runs from Putney to Mortlake on the River Thames. Starting time varies according to the state of the tides. The race can be viewed from many vantage points – bridges, riverbanks, and riverside pubs: theboatrace.org.

- SEVERAL WEEKS IN MARCH: DAILY MAIL IDEAL HOME EXHIBITION

  o Largest annual consumer home show in the world (celebrating 105 years in 2013), held at Earl's Court Exhibition Centre, Warwick Road, SW5: idealhomeshow.co.uk.

- END OF MARCH: BADA ANTIQUES AND FINE ART FAIR

  o An annual showcase for members of the British Antique Dealers Association featuring furniture, paintings, silver, glass, ceramics, jewellery and more. Carefully vetted. Held at Duke of York

Square, near Sloane Square, Chelsea: bada-antiques-fair.co.uk.

APRIL

- FIRST WEEK OF APRIL: Deadline for submitting artwork to the Royal Academy Summer Exhibition (May).

- 21 APRIL: HM THE QUEEN'S BIRTHDAY

  o Hyde Park and Tower of London. A 41-gun salute to mark the actual (not the official) birthday of HM The Queen, fired by the King's Troop Royal Horse Artillery in Hyde Park (opposite the Dorchester Hotel), and a 62-gun royal salute fired by the Honourable Artillery Company at the Tower of London (on London Wharf). The Queen's official birthday is celebrated at Trooping the Colour, a ceremony held in June.

- 23 APRIL: ST. GEORGE'S DAY

  o St. George has been the patron saint of England since the 14th century. On this day, historically, but not always in the present day, Englishmen wore a red rose in their lapels (St. George's symbol). The flag of St. George (a red cross on white background) is flown from many buildings throughout England.

- EARLY APRIL: THE GRAND NATIONAL STEEPLECHASE

- o Many consider this to be the most famous steeplechase in the world, run at Aintree racecourse near Liverpool: grandnational.fans.

- APRIL OR MAY: FA CUP FINAL

  o Climax of the English football season.

- THURSDAY BEFORE GOOD FRIDAY: MAUNDY THURSDAY

  o Held at Westminster Abbey every 10th year and at various cathedrals around the country during the other nine. The Queen distributes purses of specially minted coins to as many disadvantaged men and women as the years of her age.

- FRIDAY BEFORE EASTER SUNDAY: BANK HOLIDAY, GOOD FRIDAY

- GOOD FRIDAY: HOT CROSS BUNS SERVICE

  o In a ceremony that dates back hundreds of years, 21 widows are given money and hot-cross buns after a church service at St Bartholomew-the-Great in Smithfield, EC1.

- EASTER SUNDAY SERVICE

  o Seating at 10:00, St. George's Chapel, Windsor Castle, SL4. The Queen and the Royal Family worship together in St. George's Chapel. Visitors can attend. The queue is long, so arrive early. Many people do not enter the chapel, so do not be discouraged by the size of the queue. Contact: The Chapel Clerk, Windsor Castle, Windsor, Berkshire, SL4.

- EASTER SUNDAY PARADE

o At Battersea Park, there is a parade with colourful floats and bands. At the Tower of London, Yeomen Warders in state dress.

- MONDAY FOLLOWING EASTER SUNDAY – BANK HOLIDAY, EASTER MONDAY

- EASTER MONDAY: LONDON HARNESS HORSE PARADE

o The London Harness Horse Parade takes place annually on Easter Monday at The South of England Centre, Sussex. Steeped in tradition, the parade offers onlookers a glimpse into a world gone by and for those participating, a chance to show off their best turnouts as well as meet up with friends and fellow enthusiasts. The Parade, in its present form, is actually an amalgam of two traditional parades – the London Cart Horse Parade, which was founded in 1885, and the London Van Horse Parade, which was founded in 1904 at Battersea Park. Not frequently seen in central London, this annual Easter Monday event features **an important** parade of working horses, from giant cart horses to sturdy Shetland ponies, all pulling gorgeous old carts, carriages and engines. A vision of how London must have a looked a century ago. Tickets not required.

- LATE APRIL: THE LONDON MARATHON

o The famous London marathon is made up of competitors from around the world – marathon runners, disabled runners, those running for charitable causes, celebrities and those just out for fun. The race winds throughout many areas of

London and finishes outside of Buckingham Palace:

<u>virginmoneylondonmarathon.com</u>.

- CRICKET SEASON BEGINS: Dates vary

- SCOTTISH MILITARY TATTOO: Dates vary

   o London's Royal Albert Hall. The story of some of Scotland's heroes is interwoven with the best of Scottish (and Irish) music, song and dance. The massed pipes and drums are led by the pipes and drums of the London Regiment: <u>thescottishtattoo.com</u>.

MAY

- AFTER 1 MAY: Apply for Steward's Enclosure at Henley Regatta (June).

- FIRST MONDAY IN MAY: MAY DAY BANK HOLIDAY

- 21 MAY: LILIES AND ROSES

   o Henry VI founded both Eton College and King's College, Cambridge. Every year, on the anniversary of Henry's murder in the Tower of London, delegates from the schools place flowers on the spot of the King's death – lilies from Eton and roses from King's.

- 29 MAY: OAK APPLE DAY

   o The Chelsea Pensioners honour Charles II, founder of the Royal Hospital in Chelsea, on the anniversary of Charles II's escape after the Battle of Worcester. The King's statue is decorated with oak leaves in memory of the fact that Charles hid in an oak tree to escape his pursuers.

- LAST MONDAY IN MAY: SPRING BANK HOLIDAY

- LAST SATURDAY IN MAY, FIRST REHEARSAL: TROOPING THE COLOUR

  o Leaves from Buckingham Palace along the Mall to Horse Guards Parade, Whitehall and back again. The first of two rehearsals (the second held in June) to prepare for the actual Trooping the Colour, the second Saturday in June, in the presence of HM The Queen. A magnificent parade of colourful military units that celebrates the Queen's official birthday. Tickets required: royal.uk/history-and-traditions.

- EARLY MAY: THE BADMINTON HORSE TRIALS

  o At Badminton, Avon, Gloucestershire. International equestrian competition: Badminton-horse.co.uk.

- EARLY MAY TO SEPTEMBER: POLO SEASON BEGINS

  o At Windsor Great Park, matches are held most Saturdays and Sundays (guardspoloclub.com). London Polo Club hosts a variety of competitions in Ham, Richmond-upon-Thames: hampoloclub.com.

- MID-MAY: ROYAL WINDSOR HORSE SHOW

  o Held in Windsor, Berkshire. International show with jumping and driving, various displays and trade exhibits. It is possible to become a member for a fee that allows access to the Members' Enclosure for the week of the show: rwhs.co.uk.

- LATE MAY-EARLY JUNE: BATH FESTIVAL

  o Festival of music and arts with concerts, exhibitions, tours and lectures: bathmusicfest.org.uk.

- LATE MAY: RHS CHELSEA FLOWER SHOW

  o Held on the grounds of the Royal Hospital Chelsea, this is the world's leading horticultural event and always visited by members of the Royal Family. Tuesday and Wednesday are reserved for RHS members with admittance to the general public on Thursday, Friday and Saturday. Tickets are limited and all are sold in advance. Apply to RHS after 1 January. No children under five and no pets are admitted: rhs.org.uk/chelsea.

- LATE MAY – EARLY JUNE: HAY-ON-WYE LITERARY FESTIVAL

  o For 10 days, this small Welsh town of around 1,500 people, and some 40 bookshops, conducts a highly-important, international literary festival. The program includes authors and speakers from around the world, discussion panels and a full program for children. Prominent recent visitors include former United States President Bill Clinton: hay-on-wye.co.uk.

- MAY TO AUGUST: GLYNDEBOURNE FESTIVAL

  o Near Lewes, East Sussex. International festival of opera. Dress is formal and picnics on the lawn are the norm. The festival is popular, so book early for tickets. Special train services run from Victoria Station to Glyndebourne and return from Lewes: glyndebourne.com.

- MAY THROUGH SEPTEMBER: REGENT'S PARK OPEN AIR THEATRE SEASON

  o A full programme of plays performed outdoors, featuring all genres. Open Air Theatre, Inner Circle, Regent's Park, NW1: openairtheatre.com.

- MAY TO OCTOBER: CHICHESTER FESTIVAL THEATRE SEASON

  o A rich history of theatre making with a comprehensive programme of classic plays, musicals and premieres in Chichester, West Sussex: cft.org.uk.

- MAY TO OCTOBER: SHAKESPEARE'S GLOBE THEATRE

  o Enjoy outdoor theatre in the reconstructed Globe Theatre on the banks of the River Thames in the heart of London: shakespearesglobe.com.

JUNE

- FIRST WEEKEND IN JUNE: THE DERBY (pronounced DAR-by)

  o Held at Epsom Downs in Surrey, this is the most famous and prestigious horse race in the world. It covers one and a half miles. Created at a noble dinner party in 1779 and named after one of the diners, Lord Derby. Bookings open 1 January: epsom.thejockeyclub.co.uk.

- SECOND WEEKEND IN JUNE: POLO IN THE PARK

  o Chesterton's Polo in the Park generally takes place the second weekend in June and is a firm social fixture in the London summer social calendar. This three-day polo festival is held in Hurlingham Park, Fulham, and includes an array of entertainment and pitchside bars: polointheparklondon.com.

- 10 JUNE: HRH THE DUKE OF EDINBURGH'S BIRTHDAY

  o A 41-gun salute fired by the King's Troop Royal Horse Artillery at noon in Hyde Park (opposite the Dorchester Hotel), and a 62-gun royal salute fired by the Honourable Artillery Company at one o'clock at the Tower of London (on London Wharf). No tickets required.

- 24 JUNE: KNOLLYS RED ROSE CEREMONY

  o In the 14th century, Sir Robert Knollys was fined for building an unauthorised footbridge across Seething Lane. The fine imposed was one red rose from his garden to be given to the Lord Mayor of London every year. Today his descendants, along with the churchwardens of All-Hallows-by-the-Tower, continue the tradition. Contact: The Clerk to the Company of Watermen and Lighterman of the River Thames at Watermen's Hall, 16 St. Mary at Hill, EC3R 8EE.

- EARLY JUNE: BEATING RETREAT

  o A musical spectacle of sound and colour held on two successive evenings at the Horse Guards Parade, central London. It originated when the beating of drums and the parading of post guards heralded the closing of camp gates and the lowering of flags at the end of a day of battle. Today, it is a ceremony reserved for special occasions. The event begins with the salute being taken by HM the Queen or another member of the royal family: trooping-thecolour.co.uk/retreat.

- EARLY JUNE: BIGGIN HILL INTERNATIONAL AIR FAIR & POLO IN THE PARK

  o At Biggin Hill Airport, Kent. Jet formation aerobatics, historic aircraft rally, modern military jets and extensive ground exhibition: militaryairshows.co.uk.

- MID-JUNE, VARIABLE EACH YEAR: TROOPING THE COLOUR (THE QUEEN'S BIRTHDAY PARADE)

  o Two rehearsals are held before the official event (on the last Saturday in May and the first Saturday in June). The official event is held on the second Saturday in June. HM The Queen's Official Birthday Parade starts at 1030 hours on Horse Guards Parade. Tickets are allocated by lottery. Send a letter requesting tickets along with a self-addressed envelope (s.a.e.) between 1st January and 28th February to Brigade Major, HQ Household Division, Horse Guards, Whitehall, SW1A 2AX to receive an application. Only two tickets are allocated per successful entry. Although tickets are required for the event, it is possible to go to St James's Park or outside Buckingham Palace to get a glimpse of the Queen. The event is broadcast live on BBC1. Highlights are shown later in the day on BBC2.

- MID-JUNE, VARIES EACH YEAR: HM THE QUEEN'S OFFICIAL BIRTHDAY SALUTE

  o A 41-gun salute is fired by the King's Troop Royal Horse Artillery at noon in Hyde Park, and a 62-gun royal salute is fired by the Honourable Artillery Company at one o'clock at the Tower of London (on London Wharf). No tickets required.

- MID-JUNE: AEGON TENNIS TOURNAMENT

  o Men's tennis tournaments on grass held at The Queen's Club, West Kensington, two weeks before Wimbledon. Tickets are allocated by ballot. To access the ballot, register on the mailing list: queensclub.co.uk.

- USUALLY HELD THIRD WEEK IN JUNE: ROYAL ASCOT

  o The world's most famous horse race meeting dates to 1711. Events held Tuesday through Friday are attended by members of the Royal Family. Formal attire, hats and gloves are required for ladies and full morning suit for men if you hold tickets for specific enclosures. To obtain passes for the Royal Enclosure, contact your embassy or high commission for information regarding allocated tickets: ascot.co.uk.

- USUALLY HELD THIRD WEEK IN JUNE: QUEEN'S CUP FINAL INTERNATIONAL POLO TOURNAMENT

  o Polo is one of the fastest growing, high end sports in the UK. The Queen's Cup is held at The Guards Polo Club, Royal Windsor Great Park, Berkshire: guardspoloclub.com.

- JUNE TO AUGUST: ROYAL ACADEMY SUMMER EXHIBITION

  o At the Royal Academy of Arts, Piccadilly, W1. The Summer Exhibition is the largest open contemporary art exhibition in the world, drawing together a wide range of new work by both established and little-known living artists. Tickets may be pre-booked or purchased on the day (royalacademy.org.uk). If you are either an amateur or professional artist, you can also submit work to the Summer Exhibition.

- JUNE TO AUGUST: MEDIEVAL JOUSTING TOURNAMENTS

  o Jousting tournaments take place at various castles throughout the UK during the summer months and make for a fun day out. Visit the castle, picnic on the grounds and enjoy the jousting tournament conducted in period costume. For more information and schedule of events and venues, visit: knightsroyal.co.uk.

- LATE JUNE: ORDER OF THE GARTER CEREMONY

  o A special service marks the oldest order of chivalry in England. The Knights of the Garter gather at St. George's Chapel in Windsor Castle, where new knights take the oath and are invested with the insignia. It is attended by HM the Queen and is preceded by a colourful procession of knights wearing their blue velvet robes and black velvet hats with white plumes. A limited number of tickets is available for members of the public. Applications must be sent between 1st January and 1st March

- MID-JULY THROUGH EARLY SEPTEMBER: PROMENADE CONCERTS (THE PROMS)

  o A traditional British music festival held at the Royal Albert Hall throughout the summer (royalalberthall.com/tickets). Guidebooks are available from April, including a booking form. Note, too, that proms are held elsewhere in Britain over the summer months.

- LAST MONDAY IN JULY: SWAN UPPING

  o Swan Upping is the annual census of the swan population on parts of the River Thames. The Dyers and Vintner's Companies have the right, established in medieval times, to keep swans on the river, as does the Crown. Every year, the Queen's Swan Keeper and Swan Markers from the two livery companies row in skiffs along the river to mark the cygnets (baby swans). It is possible to view the proceedings from several pubs along the river, as well as by tour boat, which is operated by Swan Lifeline: swanlifeline.org.uk.

- LAST TUESDAY TO SATURDAY IN JULY: GLORIOUS GOODWOOD HORSERACING

  o Horse racing at one of the most beautiful courses in the world on top of the Sussex Downs. It is one of the highlights of the social summer season, famously described by King Edward VII as 'a garden party with racing tacked on': goodwood.co.uk.

- LATE JULY OR EARLY AUGUST: DOGGETT'S COAT AND BADGE RACE

o Possibly the oldest rowing race in the world, this event was begun by Irish actor Thomas Dogett in 1715 to mark the crowning of George I. Six water boatmen race against the tide from London Bridge to Albert Bridge. The prize is a scarlet livery with a large silver badge.

AUGUST

- LATE JULY/EARLY AUGUST: COWES WEEK

  o Cowes, on the Isle of Wight, is known as "the home of world yachting". This is the location of the original yacht club, the Royal Yacht Squadron. The Cowes Week sailing competition has been held every year since 1826 (outside of wartime) and is a highlight of the British summer social season. With up to 40 daily races and over 1,000 boats taking part, it is the largest sailing regatta of its kind in the world. Cowes is accessible by car or passenger ferry from Southampton: comesweek.co.uk.

- EARLY AUGUST TO THE END OF SEPTEMBER: BUCKINGHAM PALACE OPENS TO VISITORS

  o Buckingham Palace is the official London residence of HM The Queen. The Palace's state rooms and garden are open to visitors while the Queen is on her summer holidays in Scotland. Advance tickets (which will allow you to avoid some of the long queues) are available online at: tickets.royalcollection.org.uk.

- MID-AUGUST: EDINBURGH INTERNATIONAL FESTIVAL

o The Edinburgh International Festival presents a varied programme of classical music, theatre, opera and dance in six major theatres and concert halls, as well as in a number of smaller venues, over a three-week period in late summer each year. It is said to be the largest festival of the arts. For details and information, visit: eif.co.uk. Running alongside this is the well-regarded Edinburgh Festival Fringe, which features avant-garde entertainment: edfringe.com.

- THREE WEEKS IN AUGUST: EDINBURGH MILITARY TATTOO

  o One of the most spectacular shows in Britain, this military extravaganza is held on the floodlit grounds of Edinburgh Castle. Tickets sell out quickly. Bookings can be accepted as early as December of the prior year: edinburghtattoo.co.uk.

- LAST MONDAY IN AUGUST: SUMMER BANK HOLIDAY

- AUGUST BANK HOLIDAY SUNDAY AND MONDAY: NOTTING HILL CARNIVAL

  o This is the largest street festival in Europe, attracting over one million visitors a year. The spectacular two-day celebration of fun, food, culture and music began in 1965 when Trinidadian immigrants and residents of Notting Hill brought the neighbourhood people together after the race riots of the 1950s: thenottinghillcarnival.com.

SEPTEMBER

- EARLY SEPTEMBER: GREAT RIVER RACE

    o A 22-mile boat race along the River Thames from Ham, near Richmond-upon- Thames, Surrey, to Docklands. Features all manner of craft, including Chinese dragon boats, Viking longboats, whalers, dinghies, skiffs and canoes:greatriverrace.co.uk.

- MID-SEPTEMBER: HORSEMAN'S SUNDAY

    o Church of St. John and St. Michael, Hyde Park Crescent, W2. A morning service dedicated to the horse with mounted vicar and congregation followed by a procession of 100 horses through Hyde Park: stjohns-hydepark.com.

- MID-SEPTEMBER: LONDON OPEN HOUSE

    o Access to over 700 London buildings and gardens of historical and/or architectural significance. Most of these venues are normally closed to the public. Takes place over a two-day weekend. An Open House directory is available in most libraries, which lists all sites and relevant details including information on early booking for guided tours at some locations: openhouselondon.org.uk.

- MID-SEPTEMBER: MAYOR'S THAMES FESTIVAL

    o Along the banks of the River Thames between Westminster Bridge and Tower Bridge, this free outdoor festival includes art exhibitions, shows, street theatre, children's activities and music.

Thousands participate in the spectacular Night Carnival that's a mixture of fireworks, masquerade, dance, music and costume: thamesfestivaltrust.org.

- 27 SEPTEMBER OR THE FRIDAY PRECEDING: ADMISSION OF SHERIFFS

  o The livery companies of the city elect two sheriffs on Midsummer Day. Today, the new sheriffs march in a colourful procession from Mansion House to the Guildhall to be installed in office.

- 29 SEPTEMBER: ELECTION OF THE LORD MAYOR

  o In a ceremony that dates from 1546, the Lord Mayor is selected at the Guildhall then rides in state to Mansion House while the city bells ring out. Guildhall Yard: feltmakers.co.uk/election-of-the-lord-mayor-atguildhall.

OCTOBER

- SEND FOR Royal Epiphany Tickets (January).

- SEND FOR Cheltenham Hunt Meeting Tickets (March).

- FIRST SUNDAY IN OCTOBER: PEARLY KINGS AND QUEENS FESTIVAL

  o Historically, Pearly Kings and Queens were engaged in street and market trades and initially sewed found pearl buttons onto their clothing from as early as the 19th century. This gradually evolved into the full-fledged pearl costumes that we see today. The "Pearlies", as they are known, now function as a charitable organisation. The annual festival is held at St Paul's Church, Covent Garden: pearlysociety.co.uk.

- LATE OCTOBER: QUIT-RENTS CEREMONY

  o Dating back more than 800 years, the ceremony is the oldest legal act that is still performed outside of the Coronation. It is held to mark the occasion when the City Solicitor pays one of the Queen's officials (the Remembrancer) a token for the rent of properties and land leased long ago. For example, for Shropshire he pays two knives (one blunt and one sharp) and for the Forge in the Strand, he pays 61 nails and six horseshoes: informationbritain.co.uk.

- DATE VARIES, OCTOBER/NOVEMBER: STATE OPENING OF PARLIAMENT

  o English pageantry at its finest. HM The Queen rides in the Irish state coach from Buckingham Palace to the House of Lords, where she addresses both houses of Parliament from the Throne in the House of Lords. Viewing along the route. The House of Lords is not open to the public: parliament.uk.

- LATE OCTOBER/EARLY NOVEMBER: OPENING OF THE LAW COURTS

  o A closed service is held at Westminster Abbey attended by Her Majesty's Judges and Queen's Counsel dressed in state robes and wigs. Afterwards, the Lord Chancellor leads the procession from the east end of the Abbey to the

House of Lords. The first motion of the year constitutes the official opening of the Courts: parliament.uk.

- LAST SUNDAY OF OCTOBER: BRITISH SUMMERTIME ENDS

NOVEMBER

- SEND FOR the New Year's Day Parade Tickets (January).

- 5 NOVEMBER: GUY FAWKES DAY (BONFIRE NIGHT)

  o Bonfires, fireworks and burning effigies of Guy Fawkes throughout the UK on the nearest weekend to this date celebrate his failure to blow up the King and the Houses of Parliament in the Gunpowder Plot of 1605. There is a particularly spectacular event at Lewes, East Sussex. The Evening Standard and Metro newspapers publish lists of bonfires and fireworks displays in the London area in the week leading up to Guy Fawkes Day.

- 1ST SUNDAY IN NOVEMBER: LONDON TO BRIGHTON RALLY (RAC Veteran Car Run)

  o This event is open to cars built between 1895 and 1904 and commemorates the repeal of the Red Flag Laws in 1905. With over 500 cars taking part in the 60-mile run to Brighton, it is the largest gathering of old cars in the world. Departs from 08:00 at Hyde Park Corner. Pre-departure festivities and also along the route. No tickets required.

Contact The RAC Motor Sports Association Ltd., Motor Sports House, Riverside Park, Colnbrook, Slough SL3 OHG: veterancarrun.com.

- 2ND SATURDAY IN NOVEMBER: LORD MAYOR'S PROCESSION AND SHOW

  o The new Lord Mayor takes up his post in a colourful procession from Guildhall to the Royal Courts of Justice in an 18th-century gold state carriage, escorted by medieval-costumed bodyguards, elaborate floats, acrobats, trumpeters and livery companies. The route is three miles long and features over 6,500 people. No tickets required for viewing along the route: lordmayorsshow.org or cityoflondon.gov.uk.

- SUNDAY CLOSEST TO 11 NOVEMBER: REMEMBRANCE SUNDAY

  o Around the Cenotaph at Whitehall. A service is held in memory of those killed in battle since 1914. It is attended by HM The Queen, members of the Royal Family, the Prime Minister, members of the Cabinet and members of the Opposition. Two minutes silence is observed as Big Ben strikes 11:00. Similar services take place in churches in towns nationwide. During the week which precedes this event, poppies are sold to raise money for ex-servicemen. Poppy wreaths are placed at war memorials in village high streets and grave sites.

DECEMBER

- THROUGHOUT DECEMBER: HANDEL'S MESSIAH

  o Performances of Handel's Messiah during the Christmas season are staged around the UK. One outstanding production is held at St. Paul's Cathedral. Arrive early for good seats. Contact: The Chapter House, St. Paul's Churchyard, EC4: stpauls.co.uk.

- THROUGHOUT DECEMBER: CHRISTMAS CONCERTS AND CAROLS

  o At Royal Albert Hall. Various concerts to cover all tastes and ages including carols by candlelight on Christmas Eve: royalalberthall.com.

- MID-DECEMBER: Outdoor skating rinks open for the holiday season around the city – Somerset House, Marble Arch, Natural History Museum, Hampstead Heath, and more. Skates are available for hire. Tickets can be booked in advance or purchased on the day.

- MID-DECEMBER: CHRISTMAS TREE LIGHTING CEREMONY

  o At Trafalgar Square, WC2. Each year an enormous Christmas tree is donated by the people of Oslo, Norway, in remembrance and thanks for British assistance during World War II. Carol services are sung every evening beneath the tree until Christmas.

- MID-DECEMBER THROUGH MID-JANUARY: PANTOMIME

  o Held throughout Britain in local theatres between mid-December and mid-January. Traditional pantomimes feature a comedic take on a well-known fairy tale or story and are characterised by audience participation, sing-along and candy thrown into the audience. There is often a well-known actor who makes a special appearance in the leading role. Check theatre listings or local newspapers for information.

- 25 DECEMBER: CHRISTMAS BANK HOLIDAY

- 25 DECEMBER: The Queen's Christmas speech is broadcast.

- 25 DECEMBER: CHRISTMAS DAY SWIM

  o The Peter Pan Cup has taken place every Christmas Day since 1864. Members of the Serpentine Swimming Club compete in this annual race across the Serpentine in Hyde Park.

- 26 DECEMBER: BOXING DAY BANK HOLIDAY

- 31 DECEMBER: NEW YEAR'S EVE

  o Big Ben tolls at midnight. Crowds gather at Trafalgar Square and along the River Thames in central London, creating **an important** party atmosphere to ring in the New Year. Fireworks take place in several locations.

Chapter 15:

Personal

notes

Congratulations on your move to London! We hope you enjoy this book, keep it for reference and share with your friends, family, colleagues and strangers.

HERE'S TO A BRILLIANT
ADVENTURE!

The Junior League of London is the UK chapter of The Association of Junior Leagues International.

THE JUNIOR LEAGUE OF LONDON

There are 292 Junior Leagues in the US, the UK, Canada and Mexico, with over 150,000 members. Together we are one of the most impactful volunteer organisations in the world, and we're 100% powered by women!

Our mission is simple: to promote voluntary service, develop the potential of women and improve our community through the effective action and leadership of trained volunteers.

In London, our 300 members give over 10,000 volunteer hours every year. With only one part-time employee, our charity is almost entirely volunteer run. From tutoring to serving meals, our impact is significant and tangible.

To find out more or get in touch, visit jll.org.uk.

Made in the USA
Middletown, DE
27 June 2021